Swimming at Suppertime

Swimming at Suppertime

Seasons of Delight
on the Wrong Side of Buzzards Bay

Carol Wasserman

Dear Alice,
I have long admired you
and your devotion to your
church and community — What a
pleasure it is ⊙ to meet you —
fond best wishes
— Carol Wasserman

Crown Publishers
New York

Published by Crown Publishers, New York, New York.
Member of the Crown Publishing Group, a division of Random House, Inc.

www.randomhouse.com

CROWN is a trademark and the Crown colophon
is a registered trademark of Random House, Inc.

National Public Radio, NPR, and All Things Considered are federally
registered service marks of National Public Radio, Inc., and may not
be used without permission of NPR.
Some text originally created for broadcast on NPR.

Printed in the United States of America

Design by Leonard Henderson

Library of Congress Cataloging-in-Publication Data
Wasserman, Carol.
Swimming at suppertime : seasons of delight on the
wrong side of Buzzards Bay / Carol Wasserman.—1st ed.
1. Wareham (Mass.)—Social life and customs.   2. Country life—Massachusetts—Wareham.
3. Buzzards Bay (Mass. : Bay)—Social life and customs.   4. Country life—Massachusetts—
Buzzards Bay (Bay)   5. Wasserman, Carol.   6. Wareham (Mass.)—Biography.   I. Title.
F74.W28 W37 2002
974.4'82—dc21
[B]   2001047912
ISBN 0-609-60840-1

10   9   8   7   6   5   4   3   2   1

First Edition

for

R. M. W.

E. M. B.

A. H. G.

father, son, and holy ghost
blessed trinity

Contents

Introduction   11

After Labor Day   15

Aubrey   17

Mr. O'Furniture   23

Cranberries   26

The People Who Moved Here by Mistake   28

The Standing Stones   35

Before Frost   38

Doubting Thomas   40

A Real Team   43

Contents

Macouns   45

Rummage Sale   48

Vinyl   51

Widow's Exemption   56

Out Digging   58

Ghosts   61

Rutabaga Casserole   63

Afternoon Nap   66

The Food Bank   68

The Shell Dump   70

Tree of Lights   72

The Poor Relations   75

A Story from the Gospel of Luke   81

Bad Day   85

Fishing   88

Bittersweet   91

Finch Nets   94

Staying   98

Toll House Cookies   101

Contents

Winter Rentals   104

Wendell   107

Barney   110

Married In   112

Coyotes   115

Scavengers   118

Staying Home   121

Burning Brush   126

Demons   129

Sea Glass   133

The Herring Run   136

New Gardens   139

Memorial Day   142

Side Chairs   148

Men and Geese   151

June Weddings   154

The Amish   157

Little Frieda   160

Block Dance   167

Contents

Tall Ships   169

Auntie   171

The ATM   177

White Peaches   180

Therapists in August   184

The Queen Mum's Cake   187

Some Random Thoughts on the Subject of Love:
I Corinthians 13   190

Putting Something By   192

The Ladies Who Swim at Suppertime   197

Acknowledgments   201

Introduction

I HAVE LIMITED EXPERIENCE of anything beyond the tidal or political boundaries of Weweantic, Massachusetts. The sense we have, those of us who are year-rounders, is that there are better places, happier places, easier places. When the summer people roll into town they have stickers on their cars which read *Malden Catholic High School* or *The University of Virginia,* which are, for us, equally exotic and remote.

This causes us to act out, in the way of adolescents who feel awkward and ashamed. We put stickers on *our* back windows which read, "My Other Car Is A Piece Of Crap Too."

This is only a sad fiction—in truth we have no other car. We have no other house to which we might repair in the damp heat of August, no summer weekends free to lie on a rented beach. We are at work while the rest of the world is on vacation. And we are grateful for the paycheck.

But when the season ends, and the place clears out, we stay. The show folds, the circus leaves town. We hunker down on the empty benches in front of boarded-up ice-cream shops, knowing we are here for the duration.

Which, in reality, is fine with us. Although how this can be possible is a complete puzzle to the tourists and the summer people and the unfortunate few who find that they have moved here by mistake.

Swimming at Suppertime

After Labor Day

O NCE UPON A TIME you had to drive
through here to get over the Bridge. The fried clam joints and
motels and places selling plastic lobsters were boarded up in
the seventies when they finished building the interstate. What
got left behind was lots of warm clean ocean lapping at the
wrong side of Buzzards Bay.

Most of us in the trailer parks and spavined summer cottages manage to work steady in the summer. We clean the
big houses, bang nails, bag groceries. We throw compost. Bus
tables. Baby-sit. We do it six or seven days a week. Sundays are
time-and-a-half, unless you're being paid under the table. But
few of us cobble together twelve good months in any salty, fog-
blown year.

So in the ghost-town weekends after Labor Day we are

free to sit in each other's yards in the afternoon, drinking beer and watching the little kids chase each other around with squirt guns. The air smells of mildew and septic tank and piney scrub. Our teenagers stand around a rusty propane grill, cooking unnaturally pale, fatty hamburgers, eager to eat and be gone. The sun goes down. The babies fall asleep inside. We get our turn at what's left of the macaroni salad, the cheap hot dogs, the quahogs dug without a permit. There is end-of-season corn, which we assume was stolen from one of the truck farms where the real cash crop is marijuana hidden behind a wall of salt-marsh hay.

It grows dark. We swat at the tiny flies which hatch and swarm for a few days at the tag end of the year. We light cigarettes, wave the smoke away.

To the extent that we had planned our lives at all, most of this we did not plan. Our youthful expectations had been vague. The future looked like one of those off-shore islands which by a trick of light and distance floats over the water on the far horizon. Close-up, we can see it's as ordinary and terrestrial as the empty motel down the road.

But sitting in old beach chairs, our bellies full, listening to waves slapping at the high-water mark, we believe— briefly—that if the kids stay healthy, the pipes behind the sink don't freeze, and the car miraculously passes inspection, we too can make it through one more winter here of hard times and limited visibility.

Aubrey

I LOST NOTHING IN the housebreak which was not going to become supper at some point in the hard future.

I had a small box of jewelry which had been given to me over time. There was little of great value in the collection. A few old silver brooches, a thin pink gold necklace, a wedding ring which no longer meant anything to me, and a string of pearls which did. One day I came home from work to find the place ransacked, but all that anyone could find to steal was the jewelry box and a coffee-can half full of loose change which had been sitting on the warming shelf of the kitchen range.

I did, however, have a minimal amount of insurance.

Anyone who has been the object of a break-in will tell you that the worst of it is not the dispossession—it is the sense of violation. I hadn't owned much that was irreplaceable, in any event having long ago learned that there is nothing so dear that it cannot be sold to keep the lights on. Personal possessions in and of themselves are merely protein in another form, like sunlight to grass to cow to supper. This knowledge has left me hard-hearted in the face of the sufferings of those poor souls who have been separated from their collections of Sandwich glass, or Native American baskets, or Shirley Temple dolls. I suppose it must be difficult to pick up and go on if you have been unwise enough to invest your energy in accumulation. Do *things* give meaning to your labor? I had never earned enough from my labor to want anything except a way to keep disaster at bay for one more day, one more paycheck.

So I was sorry to be prematurely separated from my string of pearls, and for a few months I found myself uncharacteristically jumpy and nervous when I would hear the creaking and groaning that all old houses make in the dark. But I was eager to put this windfall, this insurance check, to good use. I wanted to hire someone to paint the bare trim on the house. It was a job I could do myself, with unlimited patience and no fear at all of extension ladders. But this seemed like a fortuitous trade-off: my grandmother's pink gold necklace which I had worn almost every day of my life—except, strangely, that one day—

for an opportunity to ease my shame at the shabbiness of my surroundings.

Which, of course, is how we met.

He was painting houses. And working cheap.

Not until a few weeks into the job did it become apparent that he was not by trade or talent a house painter. But by then we had drunk many cups of tea at my kitchen table, and I did not much care that he couldn't run a bead of black paint neatly up the window mullions, or that he couldn't keep the white paint off the weathered shingles. He could do something else quite precious and unusual—he could make me laugh until the tea ran out my nose. And, apparently, I could do the same for him. We were a messy pair.

The painting itself went slowly. He would pantomime outside the window he was working on, doing puppet shows and hilariously unconvincing magic tricks. I watched from inside the house, hoping he would never finish up and go home. How lovely it was to laugh! How long it had been!

After we had drunk rivers of sweet milky tea, we told each other our life stories. I was broke and hopeless and inept at most of the skills required to survive in the world. It had started to become difficult for me to leave the house at all—there was so much empty horizon and I had no courage to march off into the unknown. Aubrey, on the other hand, seemed to be the bravest of men. The finest and most authentic; he had washed up on the Cape, like so many others, after the shipwreck of his second divorce. After the collapse of his accounting job with an airline which had been deregulated out of existence. He had spent his golden parachute supporting his kids while he wandered across the country, looking for a way to bring order and meaning out of the smoking ruins of his middle years. Now he was painting houses.

I was awestruck. How could someone have lost so much and be so unbent, unbroken?

Now, looking back, I can see that I must also have seemed like someone in possession of one or two arcane secrets of survival. There I was, with a roof over my head, although one in serious need of new shingles and new flashing. With a kid of my own—who did not need repair. With a vegetable garden and a hive of bees and a sewing machine. Ten years separated us, and I suppose I represented all the hippie girls he had missed out on as he rode the subway from Flushing to Manhattan, carrying a briefcase, every weekday of those hippie years. At some point, midway through this hilariously attenuated paint job, after the heat had begun to go out of each golden September afternoon, I said, "Will you marry me?" It was a rhetorical question.

I look at the pictures of our wedding day. We were so hopeful and delighted, standing on a windy hill outside the Unitarian church. We did not want a ceremony; I simply recited the Robert Frost poem which ends *"I shan't be gone long—you come too."* Then we exchanged rings and signed our names. I can see, in those photographs, the walnut-sized lump on the side of his neck. But we were innocent then. I must have known what lymph nodes were, but had no reason to expect that I would soon learn to use those words in a variety of terrifying sentences.

It was almost a year before we were thrown down the stairs. A routine physical. An immediate excision. The stupor which accompanies the news that everything will be taken away from you. In six months, maybe less.

He fought against leaving me for six more years. Can you understand the enormity of that gift? He accepted treatments he did not wish to undergo, and surgeries that left him physically diminished, weakened, scarred, his lovely craggy Irish face ruined and strange. He submitted to all of it only because I refused him permission to leave. I am not sure, these years later, if this was stubborn cruelty on my part. It had taken so long for us to find each other. I was unwilling to entertain the idea that there would be no last-minute reprieve, no phone call from the hospital in Boston telling us it had all been a mistake. No embarrassed radiologist explaining that all Aub needed to plump back up was more steak and extra mashed potatoes.

But there was inexpressible, concentrated sweetness in our time together, in that long autumn of approaching death.

Time in which I was careful to store up memory enough to last until our reunion on the other shore.

That reunion on a distant beach at morning is a verity which keeps me unruffled and expectant. Imagine how hard we will laugh at all the stories we hear told in Heaven! Imagine how sweet the taste of Heaven's milky tea!

Mr. O'Furniture

E XCEPT FOR THE CRICKETS, there is exquisite silence here in the bright weeks after everyone goes home.

A pounding heat-wave accompanies the kids back to school. It holds them prisoner inside airless classrooms, their heads damp with perspiration and their teachers full of regret for having chosen—years ago—to make a bargain with the Devil. Who offered them August, July, and part of June in exchange for captivity indoors with restless children the rest of their working lives.

Then two weeks into the new school year a storm front blows through, pushing the sodden heat ahead of it and bringing in the dry lightness of September. No one thinks to fold up the lawn chairs or put the picnic table away. Everyone knows what follows hard on the heels of summer's end: sweet golden afternoons, cool nights, brilliant blue mornings when there is nothing at all in the air to cause us worry. Except perhaps the possibility that this state of grace may not continue forever. That the silence may turn mean.

But for now, there is little to do after work besides mow the lawn again, and figure out what to do with all the stupid tomatoes. The freezer is full of spaghetti sauce, the shelves are lined with rose-hip jam, the flower garden is a tired mess which would like some time off.

I run the mower once through the long grass near the marsh. Which disturbs the crickets who have been singing to us for weeks now about their manic love of this still place between heat and cold, and their longing for it to be extended into time, into eternity, until it becomes as ordinary as sunshine filtered through a maple tree. Until it becomes as humdrum as wild carrots blooming on the roadside. As familiar as the smell of apples, of hay, of seaweed after moon-tide, drying in the scrub above the high-water mark.

The summer people are gone, and we are full of gratitude—if only momentarily—to be left behind here in this place where the season of delight goes on and on. In secret.

I walk the quiet beach at two o'clock. I put my bare feet in the water, to feel the strange warmth of an ocean which has not yet had time to cool. I tell myself my favorite joke: "What's

Irish and stays outdoors all summer? Paddy O'Furniture." It is almost time for my ghosts and me to come indoors. The crickets will precede us, and eat holes in all my sweaters. I should be inside battening down the hatches.

But Mr. O'Furniture and I are not ready for that yet.

Cranberries

O NE FINE, HIGH, BRIGHT blue morning I will be surprised to see a quiet pond where one did not exist the night before. Rounding the corner by the cemetery at seven, walking early to avoid the blister heat of the first few weeks of school, I will find equipment and a crew of men assembling beside the bog which abuts the saltmarsh and runs out to the innermost reach of Buzzards Bay.

They water-pick this bog. Those of us who pass by on foot, and those who come upon it at the beginning of a long, hard commute to work in Boston, are cheered and strengthened by the sight of floating cranberries. By the beauty and inevitability of ripeness.

A *dry-picked* bog does not have this salutary effect upon the spirit. Dry-picked bogs are scraped clean by a dull, mechanical process involving helicopters which lift full crates off the ground and deposit them noisily in a pile of sand. These berries are worth more at market; the plastic bags in the grocery store two months from now will be filled with expensive dry-picked fruit.

The stuff which is churned up on a perfect day in the sweaty interstice of seasons is driven up back roads to be processed into juice at the big growers co-op in Middleboro. The economics of the thing are of no concern to me, however, and furthermore it seems ridiculous that water-picked berries are devalued by the very thing which gives us—who do not labor over them—such pleasure.

So I spend a morning watching the watery extravagance of berries rising in waves of pink and crimson to the surface of a flooded world. By lunchtime the fruit is being corralled to one end of the bog. By midafternoon, the berries are a striated island in the process of disappearing up a conveyor belt.

By suppertime the loaded trucks are gone. The street is wet. There are berries left marooned in corners where I could reach them if I chose, but I never trespass to glean fields which have already yielded up the water and the blood.

The People Who Moved
Here by Mistake

O NE OF THE THINGS which scares us, and keeps us here, is the example of our unhappy neighbors who moved here by mistake. If this could happen to them, it could happen to us—we could pick up and go, and find ourselves someplace worse than where we are now. Kosovo, perhaps, or the wrong side of Beirut. Or in a four-hundred-year-old timber house with tiny shuttered windows, which we discover, too late, is downwind of Chernobyl.

Because we know too many people who have driven down from the city on some sunny day, intending to see Cape Cod. They are carrying the big book of *Maps of Eastern Massachusetts*, bound by a sturdy red spine, which identifies them as tourists. They see that it is possible to get off the highway a few exits before they reach the bridges over the Cape Cod

Canal, and so they take the old road through the scrub pine, the road that was the main thoroughfare along the coast for a thousand years before the English arrived in town. "Oh, look at that old diner, and the abandoned Mobil station—it looks like that Hopper painting!" Of course it does. The reason why this is so may not occur to them. No one here remembers either, or cares much, as far as I can tell.

If it is autumn, they will get caught behind a lumbering cranberry truck, and if it happens to be full of wet-picked fruit, there will be water everywhere, dripping from the high box, spilling onto the street. "Oh! Cranberries!" they will say, delighted, for the first six or seven miles. Then they will become impatient, and look for a straight place in the two-lane highway where they might pass the slow load and get on with it. I like to think that one or both of them were English majors back in college, and that they would be caught short if someone told them about poor myopic John Dos Passos's car crash, right there, also passing through on his way to the Cape, smashing into the back of a slow-moving cranberry truck, killing his wife and rendering him incapable, from that point on, of writing books which were not dark and unhappy.

But all that is forgotten now, and they will not think of history or literature or art. They will think about a blueberry muffin and a cup of coffee, and so when they stop to use the bathroom and have a bite to eat, they will pick up a copy of the weekly paper from the wire rack beside the door. They will

29

slide into the dark pine-paneled booth and open the paper to the classifieds.

At which point they will see the hilarious prices of real estate here, and its proximity to saltwater.

"Downwind of Chernobyl," we would tell them if they asked. But they do not. They decide to save Cape Cod for another day, and, instead, to spend this one investigating what they believe to be their own private landfall, a secret clearing in the woods where they might relocate and live out the dream of salt and sky and unplundered resources, all of it for sale on the cheap by friendly if unsophisticated natives.

A few months later they have given up their ungodly expensive apartment near Symphony Hall, having decided one merlot-soaked night that life, that short, opaque adventure, was meant to be lived with spontaneity and brio. That the city had grown stale. They would be fools not to snap up that ram-shackle little house near the beach. A starter home, the Realtor had called it, so inexpensive that it might as well be disposable, like certain European cars.

And so they come. Move in next door or up the street, as innocent as shorn lambs who have not thought to worry about whether there is in fact someone to temper the wind.

It takes only twenty-four hours—a day and a half at most—before they realize what they have done. By then it is too late.

We amble over to say hello, to ask if they need help with

anything? We bring a paper plate of brownies and a pot of rosemary for the kitchen windowsill. They have begun to panic; we can do nothing to calm them down.

"Um, no," we have to say, "there isn't a bakery. There isn't a movie theater. No bookstore, no coffee bar, no decent Indian food." No Indian restaurants of any caliber, or Vietnamese markets, or even reliable sources of porcini mushrooms. There is an IGA up near the Laundromat, we tell them, but be careful about the sale-dates on the milk and lunchmeat. They look at us suspiciously; we can't possibly be serious. They want us to be teasing them. They hope that we are putting them through some kind of bumpkin rite of passage. That eventually we will tell them about foreign-film night at the library, and cello recitals at Town Hall.

"Oh well," we think, leaving them standing, terrified, among their packing boxes. "It happens."

The next year or so is full of purposeful activity. Their jobs are in the city; they spend most of the workweek driving back upstream like distracted salmon. Meanwhile they do what is necessary to settle in, to become part of the place, to make themselves useful. To find new friends. They are eager to share with us their expertise in historic preservation, land-use management, and the financial oversight of local government. In that first year or so they manage to save us from ourselves—without them we would have torn all the rotting gingerbread off the nineteenth-century train depot downtown, covered it with vinyl siding, and sold it to the guy who wanted to open another Dunkin' Donuts.

But this is not sufficient to calm the nerves of the people who moved here by mistake. What comes next is predictable enough. We might have employed the same strategy ourselves when we were young, for similar reasons, with similar results. They wake up one morning and all at once perceive the answer to the great unasked question: "Yes! Yes!" they say. "A baby!"

Their earnest foolishness through the production sequence can be forgiven. It is universal, regardless of your place or station. A child will fix you in the vast poorly zoned vortex of space and time, will give you focus, purpose, will cause your life to have the gravitas guaranteed only to those who are certain of leaving bereft and weeping middle-aged children at some far-off graveside service.

But the decision to have a baby greatly increases the inconvenience of the impossibly long commute to Boston. After they have hired one of us to do day care, they turn what attention they have left to the problem of a job close to home. "Good luck," we think to ourselves. Finding a decent job has been our preoccupying problem, the one which keeps us up at night: "Okay, here we are. What in hell are we going to do for money?"

Year upon year we watch ourselves grow desperate, and

yet we get no closer to the answer. Our own children become adults, and we have to watch them as they try to wrestle the same demons to the ground.

Of course, the people who moved here by mistake have resources we do not. Once it becomes obvious that there is no Montessori preschool here, no Suzuki violin teacher, not even a YMCA where they might take their infants to learn to swim, they know that it is time to go. The public schools are abysmal. The few private country-day academies are far away, and, further, there is hardly anyone around to carpool with.

And so at this point they decide to head back to Boston, to pick up the life they foolishly abandoned one fine Saturday years before.

Too late! Rent control is no more; they have been priced out of the market. They cannot go home.

But they put their house on the market anyway. Since moving in they have remodeled the kitchen and put a woodstove where an old gas space heater used to be. They hope there will be no problem finding someone to assume ownership of such a small, tidy house so near the beach. They resign, with genuine regret, from the Historical Society and the Recycling Committee, and the Open Space Planning Commission. And in an act of inspired compromise, move over the bridge to one of the better towns on-Cape. Where they can finally relax and begin their lives in earnest.

On the day of their leaving we bring them a paper bag of

yellow daylily tubers dug up from our garden, for the new house, to say goodbye. We are sorry that it did not work out for them here. We never thought it would.

We wish them well, and godspeed to their children. Who will not be from here after all.

The Standing Stones

S OME YEARS AGO NOW, newly arrived from the city, Aubrey made an astonishing discovery: a tiny Stonehenge in the woods beside the neolithic coast road since renamed Route 28. Although he had been born in Brooklyn, it was a close call. Much of what his parents brought with them from Northern Ireland remained in his speech and imagination. And it did not seem implausible to him that there should be Druids in the wilds of Plymouth County.

So, seeing dolmen stones in a circle beside the road, he thought to call the State Archaeologist with the happy news.

There was great excitement in the offices of the State Archaeologist. Ever since Colonial times there have been rumors of standing stones in the woods of southeastern Massachusetts. For almost four hundred years people have been looking for what they know must be here somewhere—a sacred circle, a Celtic outpost, hard evidence of early ocean crossings in wee open coracles.

New England is full of shadows and mysteries, of course. Several miles upstream from a river near the Rhode Island border sits Dighton Rock. It is an otherwise unprepossessing hunk of glacial deposit into which are carved undecipherable glyphs. The Pilgrim Fathers believed them to be an extinct form of written Hebrew—the poor Pilgrims expected to find the Lost Tribe of Israel camped out around every new corner. Later generations believed the inscriptions to have been made by visiting Vikings, or medieval Irish monks, or perhaps Portuguese explorers sometime before the late arrival of that publicity-hungry boatload of dissidents from Holland. No one knows.

But the State Archaeologist *did* know what a circle of standing stones would look like, and was pleased to hear that some of the top stones were still in place. It did not matter, apparently, that this ring was not as large as Stonehenge. A small simulacrum would indicate a tomb site, rather than a place for public gathering. A team of specialists was hurriedly dispatched to catalog the site, sent down Route 28 in the first cool days of coppery autumn.

A week later we received a phone call from Boston. Now there was great *anger* in the offices of the State Archaeologist, the kind of fury which follows great disappointment: these were not Druid artifacts. They were stone benches, all that remained from in front of a defunct Dairy Queen, torn down years before. They wanted to know if this had been some kind of mean-spirited joke.

Ah well.

Aub does not have a headstone yet. I worry about this sometimes. But on certain aching gold afternoons near the equinox I make myself a tuna fish sandwich and drive up Route 28 to the standing stones. Where I sit and eat my lunch, while marking the position of the setting sun.

Before Frost

THE WINDOWS OF MY frail antique house are still open at night, even though I need three quilts to stay warm. We haven't had a frost yet, so the darkness is filled with the noise of crickets, stupid from the cold, sawing away in wet grass.

I have lived most of my life in this little house. It was built sometime before 1734, in what was then one of the southern-most neighborhoods of the colony of Plimoth. It's a tiny weather-beaten shingled half-Cape. The five fireplaces and the beehive oven and the hand-forged latches are intact. Everything else has suffered three centuries of decline at the hands of dampness, squirrels, and short money.

It is a fragile, sinking, lovely old wreck of a place, which I have come to confuse with my own flesh.

What occupies me now on cold nights in October, as I wait to be overtaken by sleep, are thoughts of all the things which I have left undone.

Improvident, the summer gone, I didn't get around to painting the bare cornerboards and eaves of the house, where ancient wood is exposed to the elements. The gardens are overgrown. The lilacs need to be pruned. The old trellis which holds up a rosebush—a variety named "Climbing Queen Elizabeth"—is rotted and askew, although the Queen has just set two fat buds.

I haven't stacked the firewood. I haven't scrubbed the salt and dust and pollen off the kitchen floor. I haven't steeled myself for a trip to the cellar with a clean furnace filter.

All the pumpkins and paper sacks of apples for sale on the back roads are proof that someone else's crops are gotten in. Somebody's fields have been plowed under, somebody's cranberry bogs scraped clean of fruit.

My own modest charge—this house, this saltmarsh acre—waits for me to wake up and get busy with the chores which must be done, regardless of the fact that I alone am left to mow and rake and paint and scrub. I live in the company of silence. But when I finally shut the windows against the early dark, I want there to be clean sheets and the back door hung with speckled Indian corn.

Doubting Thomas

WILL EVIL TRIUMPH?

I don't give this particular old question much closet space. Least of all while I am baking pies.

Thomas, in the Essene caves, believed that there is always celestial warfare going on, and he was inclined to think the good guys might not win. Poor Thomas. He lived where it was hot and parched. He never saw the coast of Massachusetts in the fall. He never opened up a trunk of woolen shirts and pants, stored away all summer, never washed them in a bucket of cold water before laying them on the grass to dry. He never forked up ribbons of dried seaweed, silvery and light, from the rocks which are meant to show where the public beach stops and private property begins, except that there is no such thing in Massachusetts as a private beach, and one may walk freely anywhere. He never filled the trunk of his car with seaweed, never drove home smelling like three-day-old fish in order to mulch down the garden beds.

He was without knowledge of the tree of fruit. And so could not have understood the first piecrust of apple season, which rolls out white and fragile on the surface of my kitchen table. Had no way to know how carefully I lift it into a well-worn ten-inch pie plate. How I fill the thing with hard new Greenings or a pile of Northern Spies which have been peeled and cored and sliced and, finally, tossed with sugar and a few good shakes of nutmeg and some cinnamon. Then laid down as rapidly as a hand of fortune-telling cards.

He didn't know about the pea-sized hunks of good cold butter which I drop onto the lumpy mountain. He could not have guessed about the way I cover it with the second crust.

It is possible that darkness may overcome the world. That pestilence or famine or plain old garden-variety despair may turn out the lights. But before that happens I will have pinched the edges of my piecrust shut, and poked them to form ocean waves. I will have used the tines of a dinner fork to make patterns of geese in flight across the top, to let the steam escape.

I will have covered the edges with tinfoil to protect them from the oven's heat.

And while the juices bubbled in the crust, and the room

filled with the smell of seaweed mulch and apples, I will have taken Gnostic Thomas, Doubting Thomas, who could not believe what he had not seen with his own eyes, and settled him down at my kitchen table. In Elijah's chair. And waited for him to ask: "Do you maybe have some vanilla ice cream for the top?"

A Real Team

I DROVE UP TO Mass General for one of my routine visits to the oncologist. My time there as a patient in this Harvard teaching hospital is as close as I ever came to being part of The Great University itself. For reasons having nothing to do with my own merit, I was allowed to graduate. And move on.

Now I'm just an old alumna who comes back to her alma mater for the home games. I'm not part of the drama of the place anymore; there's a new crop of freshmen. But because this is an office specializing in the treatment of what is ordinarily a geriatric cancer, the new kids have thirty years on me. As a result I have the odd sense that time runs backwards here.

It is a place of remarkable civility and good cheer. The prints on the wall are genuine, the magazine rack holds museum exhibition catalogs, and there is a big basket of candy bars.

The only jarring note, this visit, was the presence of a new young receptionist, whom I hold responsible for the lapse in judgment which the Halloween decorations represented. The office was infested with smiling ghosts and witches and spiders, like some hideous opportunistic infection. And the chemotherapy room was not improved by the addition of Things That Go Bump In The Night.

Nevertheless, Henry and Morris, two of the elderly new kids, greeted each other collegially, and made the sort of small talk which signaled their awareness of the presence of the real angel of death. Henry had not slept in two nights, he told us. He was too excited about the Red Sox, who have made it to the pennant race this year.

"Yeah," Morris said, "they're a real *team.*"

"A real team," said Henry, "Like in '49."

Morris put his overcoat and his felt hat down in the chair next to me, and asked, "So Mo Vaughn is gone—so what?! He wasn't the whole team. No one man is the whole team."

"That's right," said Margaret, the chemo nurse, as she walked him into a sunny room full of goblins and IV drips and grimacing cardboard scarecrows. "So—which arm do you want to use today?

"We're going to win this," he says. "They're a real team."

Macouns

TWO ANCIENT FARMHOUSES FACE each other across one of our country roads. They remind me of an old married couple who long ago stopped talking to each other, but remain together out of habit and their mutual need for a daily dose of unpleasantness. It is a mixed marriage— one farm family is white, the other is not. This isn't important to most people around here. But it remains very important to them.

These two small farms—sixty precious acres, give or take—grow identical crops of locally beloved Macoun apples, which they sell from competing farm stands on opposite sides of the street. All Macouns are hard and tart. They're not much good for pies, but are a fine eating apple, an eighty-year-old hybrid cross of two strong varieties: the McIntosh and the Jersey Black.

Since my palate is not acute enough to tell which side of the street an apple comes from, my choice of orchard on any given day depends on whether I am going or coming.

I stopped yesterday on the outbound side, behind a line of huge bright school buses, and a flock of little kids flapping around under the apple trees. The first grade had come for tractor rides in the sunny sharp wind. They had come to pick some apples and pet the goat and chase each other around in the dizzying apple-scented morning.

Our first-graders are pretty much all the same size, but they come in a happy variety of shapes and colors. We ourselves are a pretty mixed bunch. We take it for granted that what we look like now is what America will eventually look like, if everything goes the way it should.

I bought a nice-looking bunch of Macouns for four dollars. The pleasant woman who took my money slipped a couple of extra apples into my paper bag, in the traditional way. But when I asked if she had any cider, the smile faded and her face went as blank and hard as granite.

So I crossed the street, into the silence of the farm on the homebound side, which does not offer tractor rides or tethered goats or any of the other carnival foolishness which they regard with suspicion and contempt. They were happy to provide me with some fine unpasteurized cider made from apples grown within shouting distance of the wild Atlantic. But they had seen this particular chicken cross the road, and wanted to know why. Why would I buy my Macouns someplace else, when they could sell me better apples at a better price? Didn't a savings of twenty-five cents mean anything to me?

Didn't I know that my bag of apples from those people across the street would be fine on top, but the ones underneath would be rotten?

Then the proprietor began to lecture me about the fragile economics of an apple orchard. About how you could plant a hundred Macouns and wait years for them to reach maturity and you still wouldn't get any fruit. And did I know why this was?

To his consternation I knew exactly why, and told him so. Cross-pollination. Even if you don't intend to bake pies you still have to plant some different kind of apples nearby in order to make everything work. He didn't have any pie apples for sale, and told me darkly that maybe somebody else did.

I carried my sweet Macoun cider out into the crisp morning, across the narrow expanse of country road to the heart-lifting sight of a bumper crop of assorted new varieties of little apple-cheeked first-graders. Running around and screaming, so full of hybrid vigor.

Rummage Sale

THE RUMMAGE SALE SEASON opens this week.

I show up at as many of them as I can—we all do. But I seem to be the only one whose purpose is to paw through the boxes underneath the folding tables where they put the stuff which no one but me seems to want or love.

Rummage sales are held in the church basements of Plymouth County twice a year—once in October, after the summer people have gone home and will not be elbowing us out of the way in our shameless scramble for each other's old clock radios and faded nylon drapes and corroded muffin pans, and again in April. They are not advertised, of course. If you happen to see the sign out front, which may or may not go up a few days ahead of time, you make a note to be there when it opens. You will not read about it in the *Boston Globe,* or even in the New Bedford paper, nor will there be flyers in any out-of-town grocery store windows.

Nevertheless, our rummage sales are well-attended day-time events which have the cheerful, competitive feel of a fishing derby. We start lining up outside the door of the Congregational church a good half hour before they intend to let us in. This gives us a chance to stand around and chat, to find out who got accepted into college, who got laid off at the Ocean Spray plant, and who has decided she is too old to drive.

Eventually they open the doors, and we flood in, hearts pounding, dazzled by the sight of so much stuff heaped up, and all of it in our price range.

But what I look for at rummage sales, while everyone else is grabbing at the Tupperware and sets of dinner plates for three, are the abandoned sewing projects which are usually in a carton on the floor beneath the heap of old gravy-stained tablecloths. Henry Thoreau, in one of his cranky diatribes against his Walden Pond neighbors, says, "Think also of the ladies of the land weaving toilet cushions against the last day, not to betray too green an interest in their fates! As if you could kill time without injuring eternity!" He didn't think much of women's work, apparently, or understand the pleasure one derives from the sight of a basket of crocheting, waiting on the floor beside the sofa.

As for the cartons underneath the linen table, there is, for me at least, no sense of the work having been interrupted by death. The women who began these things—the sweaters, braided rugs, the aprons, afghans, the day dresses cut from thin, cheap printed cotton—may in fact be sleeping now in their eternal rest. But it is more likely that they are simply moving to Senior Housing. Cleaning out their closets and going through the stuff which accumulated under the beds in the spare room, shoved out of sight in haste and then forgotten.

I assume that they are giving away the things which they began and then set aside, having thought that someday they would find the time to finish up. Or lose a couple pounds to make the waistband fit.

Either way, they have let go. Left me to carry home the bags of yarn and rickrack and the pink flowered blouses which have not yet had the sleeves set in. Left me to put the tissue pieces back into the pattern envelopes. Left me to purchase for ten cents the complex feeling of obligation, gratitude, and relief that I still have time, in the darkness after supper, to finish what they started.

Vinyl

T HE POET SAID, "IN Heaven it is always autumn." Strangely, when I remember the distant past—and a disastrous early first marriage—it takes place entirely in a world of scarlet swamp maples and cold nights and the queasy knowledge that things are about to change.

The few happy memories of that otherwise dark time involve trips to the dump in the endless October of what I have chosen to remember: Saturdays with a very, very young husband, a Volkswagen bus, the riotous plenty of an old-fashioned pit full of burning trash and household goods. And a bottle of white wine.

I had no particular taste for white wine, and the young husband, as I later found out, had no particular taste for me. But on those long-ago weekends, wading into the smoking piles of Eastlake Victorian bedroom sets and wooden boxes full of blue glass canning jars with lead screw tops, I felt an irrational exultation. As if I could reconstruct a lost, discarded Eden from those grave goods which ended up far enough from the flames for us to wade in and pull them out. We'd put scavenged brass beds and soapstone sinks and little spool-legged washstands into the back of the pink-and-cream bus, take a swig of wine, and walk the perimeter of the pit again, on the lookout for new arrivals.

At that time in history—the early nineteen-seventies—it was considered ill-mannered to stand near the open trunk of someone else's car while they unloaded at the dump. This is no longer true. But in the dear distant past we were discreet. We feigned inattention, pretending to be looking for a replacement sprocket for our English Raleigh bicycle, or a heating element for the stove, when in fact we were watching carefully for *antiques*.

The word has since come to have ugly connotations. Antiques have become nervous, speculative commodities. They are nicely conspicuous, a good place to store some of the extra which has been accumulating in almost everybody's paychecks. We didn't give a fig back then about their street value—it seemed obvious and logical to us that if things were on the dump they must be worthless in the ordinary sense. But useful to anyone who had ideas about time travel and intentional simplicity.

I took these old things home because I believed I could use them alchemically. I believed it might be possible, given enough old chinaware and hooked rugs and kerosene lamps, to reconstruct a world in which I could bear to live. I had married too young, and not wisely. My great-grandmother's world, I reasoned, must have been less painful. Full of quiet afternoons when nothing was required of her except that she put up thirty quarts of pickles, and get supper on the table for a large family and the hands who lived with them on the stone-walled dairy farm.

Whose great-grandmother was this exactly? And whose farm? I had no idea, and it didn't matter.

The young husband and I would come home from the dump at closing time, and set up our smoky treasures in the yard. We'd hose off the worst of the mold and grime, then sit outside in the light of the setting sun, listening to music from speakers balanced on a windowsill. Vinyl records. Scratchy, expensive, and as necessary to us as news from home. We were exiles, and the records which accumulated in the little living room of the rented house made us feel that perhaps we had not cut ourselves off entirely from the noise and tumult of our generation.

Eventually, inevitably, we parted ways. Life began to make sense again for both of us. Sometimes leaving is a mercy.

Of course memory is a slippery fish. Memory must wiggle away from us and disappear or we would give up and die from sorrow and exhaustion. After the dark time, I sold everything of value which was left behind, and took the rest to the Salvation Army, in hopes that they might turn my outgrown life into soup for someone else. I sold the needle lace pillowcases. I sold the fancy painted dressers. Dealers came and hauled away tin bathtubs and ancient threadbare oriental rugs made by tribes which had been exterminated during the First World War. I gave away the dishes and the punched-tin kitchenware.

And I gave away the records because I could not listen to them without weeping. And because they had fallen out of fashion, anyway.

Eventually I forgot almost everything about those years. I became the recipient of several miracles. A kid. A new husband. A life as sweet as bay scallops in October.

Then recently, on a cool windy fall day, I found myself on the way to a rummage sale which draws me because of the odd mix of smells and noise. I was going for the music—a clarinet and trombone and upright piano, and three guys playing the Benny Goodman songbook. And the cozy onion cloud of corn chowder and good homemade chicken pie which drifts over the tables of used clothing and newly antique computers and their quaint peripherals.

I hadn't intended to buy anything. But found when I got home that I was carrying fifteen pounds of thirty-year-old vinyl records—all the albums I had once owned and then discarded. They were in perfect condition. Beautifully cared for.

Beautifully preserved. Someone else my age had just gone through a hard divorce.

I looked at the pile of vinyl on my kitchen table, and then was hit with it—the awful revulsion and remorse. What had I been thinking? What had made me drag home these reminders of my time in exile and the dark years after?

And why, dear god, would I want a turntable in my parlor, more wire, another obsolete format?

Why would I want the sounds of distant weeping, scratchy and familiar, when I have the clean silence of happy memory and the assurance of reunion in a place where live music is provided by an angel band.

Widow's Exemption

THE PHONE RANG THIS morning. It was the Assessor's Office. They were calling to remind me that it's time to come down and sign the papers for my Widow's Exemption.

The Widow's Exemption is a small traditional kindness which knocks seventy-five dollars off my property taxes each year. All that is required is that I show up to apprise them of my financial situation. And one other thing.

I get in the car and go down to our grand, crumbling Town Hall. The place needs a lot of repair, but every time the warrant comes up at town meeting to have the building painted and made more easily accessible to people in wheelchairs, the voters say *NO!* I suppose I should feel responsible, in part, for the limited amount of money which the town has to spread around in the form of latex paint, but there it is. I park next to the empty spaces reserved for the Selectmen, and walk into the dark baked-bean-smelling stairwell, which leads down to the Shellfish Warden's Office and up to the auditorium where the Council on Aging is serving lunch, and to the Assessor's Office, where they are waiting for me.

I've been coming in for years now, and I know my part in this little vaudeville act. The real estate agents who are sitting at the folding tables in the hall, pouring over site maps and tax records, will pretend not to listen as I walk up to the window and give my name. The women in the Assessor's Office know who I am, of course, but it is part of the routine. I say, "I'm here to sign my Widow's Exemption." As I get out my checkbook, to show them the balance in my check register, one of the good-natured clerks will say to me, in a voice loud enough to be heard by the Realtors and contractors and citizens milling around in the hallway, "We usually wait until Christmas week to do these, but we wanted to get them out of the way early this year." She winks at me conspiratorially.

Because it is now my turn to perform the Big Finish. She slides a paper across the worn wooden counter. I look at it for a second, pretending to be searching for loopholes. Then I say, in a loud and serious voice, "Yup, he's still dead."

I sign with a flourish, and walk back down the stuffy hallway, smiling, and out to the sun-filled parking lot.

Out Digging

ONE MORNING YOU WAKE up and un-
derstand that if you wish to have flowers next year, you will find
the time before work to dig your dahlias and geraniums out of
the ground. Otherwise they will freeze, and next spring, when
you are just as broke as you are now, there will be nothing
saved over to put back into the empty garden.

It's a good job to do before you've had your shower. No
one cares if you are in the yard in your pajamas, bent low, grub-
bing around with a trowel, pulling plants out of the dirt and
throwing them into an old dishpan. You can scrub your finger-
nails clean while the conditioner is in your hair, and leave the
dishpan full of uprooted greenery on the kitchen table until
you get home again.

Later, in the early dark, you can spread the table with

newspapers, and get down to the work of shaking the dahlias free of sand. You will cut the withered tops back and throw the bulbs into a paper bag. The conscientious souls in the Garden Club would have remembered to sort their bulbs by color before they got dressed for work—if they had to work at all— but you are satisfied merely to have gotten yours indoors before they were lost to a good hard frost. So, while the Garden Club Ladies would also have saved the varietal name and a description of the color and bloom time, you merely take a Magic Marker and write "Dahlias" on the grocery bag.

And put them on the floor of the back hall closet, where they will not freeze over the winter. You will not freeze either, but both you and the dahlias will be kept nicely chilled.

Then you start in on the geraniums, which you love like children. Uncomplaining, spindly children, who do not mind that they are being sent to bed for the winter. You shake the sand from their roots, too, then tie a length of white string around the sturdiest part of each main stem. You line them up like a lunatic choir. The salmons, the pinks, the precious delicate white zonals. Everybody ready?

Down into the basement, with a flashlight and great bravery. You fish around until you find the trouble light which someone left near the furnace decades ago, and turn it on. You find a dry place to put down your dishpan full of weary geraniums. Then start to tie them, one by one, upside down onto the copper pipe which feeds the outside faucet. They hang there, upended, confused for a few minutes; then they understand that they are being given a rest in a nice dark place, beyond the reach of mice.

While you are down there, you think to shut off the valve to the outside faucet, so that the line will not burst later. You wish your geraniums a pleasant sleep and happy dreams, then scuttle upstairs.

On your way past the outside faucet, you remember to open it up to let the last of the water out into the plundered garden.

You shower once again, this time to get free of some unnameable thing which lives in a dark corner of the basement where the foundation stones are caving in. You scrub the sand and dirt out of your hair and hands again, and go to bed, wishing that your own deep needs were as simply met as those of your poor dear dahlias and geraniums.

Ghosts

I

T IS NOT THE presence of ghosts, but rather their absence which haunts us.

There is something hopeful and proprietary in the stories of apparitions pacing the floorboards of old houses. A new young neighbor tells me about *her* ghost-in-residence: "She's very thin, and she wears a long white dress that kind of flutters around her." Apparently this Pre-Raphaelite specter hovers above the stairs, near the second-floor landing. My neighbor believes it to be the disembodied spirit of the previous occupant of the house.

Perhaps. But the place was lived in by *two* unmarried sisters, whom I knew well. Neither Margaret nor Janet seemed, in life, to be the sort of woman who would enjoy hovering. And certainly would not have been caught dead in anything diaphanous.

Margaret, sensible and generous, was a social worker who dressed in tweed suits and brown tie oxfords. Her sister Janet, a shy, sweet woman who was made slightly ditzy from the old anticonvulsants which used to be given to epileptics, wore navy blue sneakers with *her* tweeds, and reminded me of Harpo Marx.

So I am doubtful about my neighbor's claims of ecto-plasm in the upstairs hall. The sightings, in which she takes such pride and pleasure, are uncharacteristic of the earthly behaviors of my old friends. And unlikely in the remodeled, vinyl-sided chaos of a house full of husband and children and a couple of golden retrievers.

I, on the other hand, wait as those who have some work-ing knowledge of loss must, for a rattle in the darkness. For a curtain to lift when there is no wind. For the sound of our name called lovingly from a great distance. We who have been parted by death wait anxiously for a sign. For the comfort of the unex-plained.

Doesn't love abide?

Shouldn't there be ghosts?

Rutabaga Casserole

I'VE JUST SPENT SEVERAL days in darkness because of rutabaga casserole.

I am fond of rutabaga, or at least I believe that I am. So I was surprised and pleased to find little vacuum-packed plastic bags of the stuff all cut up nicely into half-inch cubes, parked next to the iceberg lettuce in the grocery store downtown.

If you live alone, one of the compensating pleasures of your unnatural condition is the freedom you have to eat nothing but peanut-butter crackers and diet grape soda for weeks at a time. Without a family, there is no reason to adhere to the trinitarian requirements of the Food Pyramid for plates of meat, starch, and green vegetables.

But occasionally I miss the smell of cooking, the steam and fragrance of homemade supper, which used to be routine here. And so I bought a bag of rutabaga and a can of condensed cream of mushroom soup, to make the rutabaga casserole recipe printed on the back of the lumpy bag.

Darkness comes earlier, as you have no doubt noticed, in this strange month after we set the clocks back. My instincts in November are primitive ones. Turn on the lights. Close the curtains against the wind. Mix some root vegetables with condensed soup and set a covered dish of the stuff to bake for an hour at three-fifty.

But I keep forgetting about the condition of my wiring and my third-hand stove. I forget that it is not possible to run all the lights *and* the washing machine, or the washing machine *and* the furnace. An electric blanket and the TV, if the coffee pot is plugged in. And I forgot that the oven draws more juice than my old service can provide.

The rutabaga casserole was barely warm before the house lights began flashing like the special effects in a cheesy horror film. The telephone rang once, then went dead. I spent some time hoping that this was part of an alien abduction—being sucked up by a well-maintained UFO would greatly simplify my life.

Eventually I went into the cellar with a flashlight to reset the breakers. But the house remained dark, and it began to rain, and I was left alone to think about the putrefying frog whose swollen corpse I had almost stepped on heading back up the stairs.

For several days, then, until someone came to jerry-rig the wires back together, I was thrown back six or seven generations to a time when there was nothing much to do alone in the evening except watch the horizon grow dark, watch the entertaining outlines of the locust trees disappear. It is impossible to sew a button on by candlelight, difficult to read or write. A cheerful fire in an open hearth must be banked before you go to sleep, at which point all the warm air rushes up the chimney and you wake under your blankets in the cold.

There is nothing much to do in the darkness except think about the distance between yourself and the women six or seven generations back, who in your circumstances would have been handed off permanently to brothers or sons for safekeeping. Or sent to the poorhouse, where they would have spent long days chopping whole barrels of rutabaga into half-inch cubes.

There have been perhaps four hundred thousand human generations. And only four or five in which a woman like yourself could survive alone. Could expect to be left undisturbed, in silence and solitude, to sleep without fear in her dark house, waiting for dawn and a decent electrician.

Afternoon Nap

THE DARKNESS COMES EARLIER every day now, but my afternoon nap is unaffected by the change. There is a slow, heavy stretch of time at the shank end of the day, when those of us who are unencumbered by youth or full employment curl up on the sofa and sleep. While everyone else is laboring in some vineyard, we are dozing in the weak sunshine of two o'clock. Dead to the world. You would like us to feel shame, but we do not.

You assume that we are sleeping to avoid the time of day when—decades ago—the school bus would disgorge our babies at the street, and we would meet them in a warm kitchen which smelled of oatmeal cookies. You think that just because those babies are now adult men and women who work at computer terminals in distant cities, we must fill up the time with sleep.

Or that we block out the hours when we once would have been scurrying around, making supper. That because there will not be a wreath of faces around the table tonight, we let ourselves fall into kind unconsciousness.

This is what you imagine, but it's not like that.

We are the Mothers Emeritus.

And because we are no longer keepers of the hearth, our understanding of what needs vigilance and care has expanded to include the world into which *you* have disappeared. You don't need clean socks, or help with algebra, or a ride home from your after-school job anymore. We are now off-duty in the afternoon.

When we wake up, it is growing dark. We turn on the lights, and the radio. We make ourselves a cup of tea.

Later we will be awake, when you are exhausted and asleep in your beds. We will be up past midnight, alone, listening to what we assume is the Vatican's shortwave signal from a relay transmitter somewhere in South America. We will be sitting in a pool of yellow light from a chairside lamp. Listening through the static to the voices of women singing in Latin, praying the world through the darkness.

The Food Bank

THERE IS A NOTICE in the window of the
IGA, asking for donations of food from people who are closing
up their summer cottages and pulling their boats out of the
water. Anything left in kitchen cabinets over the winter would
be eaten by mice, and canned goods would rupture after
Christmas when it's cold enough to freeze saltwater in the
harbor.

So when the last hardy souls come down to the seashore
in November's thin sunshine, to spend a weekend crawling
under the house to drain the pipes, many of them load up cartons of food and drop them off at the fire station on their way
out of town.

The ones with boats clean out their galleys, or leave
instructions at the yacht yard. Before the rigging is stripped,

before the bilges are pumped, before the hull is shrink-wrapped in blue plastic and set in a cradle out behind the sheds, someone goes below and makes a collection of all the seagoing staples left behind on dry land. And someone loads a pickup truck with the stuff and drives it down to the food bank.

The food bank is in an old cinderblock building on Route 28, hidden behind scrubby pines. It is a project of the parish, but no questions are asked about our affiliations or our beliefs. One Saturday morning a month, anyone who is hungry, or anyone who has run out of food stamps before they have run out of month, can get a paper sack of groceries to tide them over. The volunteers smile at us, underneath a portrait of a priest famous for his kindness to lepers, and ask us if we prefer the can of peas or the can of corn. They give us a bag of carrots, five pounds of flour, and some elbow macaroni. They are pleased when they have chickens to distribute, or tomatoes from someone's garden.

But at this time of year, of course, we find when we get home that there are bottles of cocktail onions underneath the store-brand cornflakes; candied ginger and maraschino cherries and tins of sardines. We have no idea what we will do with these strange little luxuries.

But we do know that they spent the summer on someone's boat, rocking in the protected chop of Buzzards Bay.

The Shell Dump

W E WAIT A COUPLE of weeks past the
opening of scallop season in the fall, and then drive out to the
shell dump to pick over the new arrivals, looking for unbroken
pairs.

We take the road that goes past the old landfill, where the
Little League field is now. All over America, kids are learning
to play baseball on places like this—the suspiciously lofty
open-air heights—remote, nicely seeded—where we used to
throw our garbage and newspapers and half-empty cans of
house paint.

We drive past the town compost yard, an unattended collection area inside a chain-link fence, where leaves and grass
clippings try their best to decompose inside of plastic trash
bags.

We keep our eyes open for a small clearing surrounded by bayberry bushes, in a ditch beside the road. And the heap of oyster, quahog, mussel, and scallop shells drying in the sun.

There's enough meat left on the fresh ones to raise quite a stink on a warm day. We do not go on warm days.

We wait until late November, when we are feeling pressured by the promises we made to the Friends of the Library or the Historical Society or the Garden Club, whose Christmas fairs are coming up. We have committed ourselves to gluing pairs of nice clean scallop shells over each white bulb on several strings of Christmas lights. Or we have volunteered to paint whales and angels and sailing ships onto the smooth inside surfaces of quahog shells. To dress them up a bit.

But first we have to bring the smelly things home, and set them in a bucket of bleach beside the back door. We let them sit for a few days until they lose their stench. We scrub them clean. Then go about the work of improving them with gold paint and glitter and tiny plastic stars. We add Santas, and miniature polystyrene fruits, and artificial rosebuds.

Then we line them up on paper-covered folding tables, next to tins of clumsily frosted cookies.

And sell them to each other at the fair.

Tree of Lights

O UTSIDE THE LIBRARY, ON a little
patch of wet lawn beside the entry doors, sits the Hospice Tree
of Lights. It's been up since just after Thanksgiving. Every year,
when the first heavy wet snowflakes fall onto warm ground,
volunteers set up a small evergreen in a bucket of cement, and
harness the thing upright with lengths of clothesline staked to
the ground. Later, two or three ladies return with a string of
white lights, and hang the tree with names of the dead.

It's a fund-raiser. The tree sits there into January. By then
it's been knocked over a few times by kids from the high school
who should know better. The volunteers come set it back up.

It slows me down as I make my way out the door of the
library with my arms full of new books and last month's maga-

zines. I'm surprised at how many of the names on the tree are familiar. I had forgotten why I don't see these people around town anymore.

At some point before the thing is hauled off to the dump, I will be the recipient of some well-intentioned thievery. A friend, seeing Aubrey's name written in red Magic Marker on a scallop shell, will slip the thing into her purse.

She thinks I will be pleased to have this souvenir. She imagines that I save up these memento mori, and unwrap them when the sky spits snow, decorating the parlor fireplace with a string of these remembrances. She thinks that at the cold beginning of the year I will want to contemplate the lengthening distance which this eternally growing collection represents.

I suppose it is possible that I have been assigned the job which museum curators took upon themselves during the long hard Siege of Leningrad, when all the paintings were taken down and sent into hiding. Maybe I have been left behind to walk starving people through the empty galleries in winter, and talk the well-loved pictures back into their frames.

But endless sorrow is not what we owe the dead. It is not, in any event, what I owe Aubrey. He would think it damn disrespectful. Unworthy of our shared belief in the healing and redemptive power of a cheap laugh.

So I throw the scallop shells away. And try to reconstruct a life where I might find myself dancing till dawn. Drinking champagne sent to my table by one of a gaggle of gentlemen admirers who trail me around adoringly.

I am his proxy here. And duty-bound to live for both of us, on the inheritance he left me, of sanity, health, and inexplicable good cheer.

The Poor Relations

THEY JUST SHOW UP one desultory rainy day in November, without anyone seeing them arrive: raggedy old Santas tied to the lampposts on Main Street. They hang like desperate temps, hands raised in greeting, each of them in a dirty faded suit of shredded plastic. None of us remembers a time when they did not appear unbidden, and stay unwanted until February.

Christmas is a desperate season here, and no one knows why the Municipal Maintenance Department feels the need to extend the time we are forced to look at these reminders of another load of obligations which we will fail to meet.

But the dirty old raggedy-ass Santas go up and stay up. We try not to see them when we come to town. The crowded crèche in front of the Selectmen's Office does not bother us as much. The wounds which it inflicts are only to those guarantees of Freedom From Religion which are so widely honored in the breach. Baby Jesus, lying there in his cement manger, surrounded by his cement parents and cement farm animals and the rest of his cement constituency, protected by a peeling plywood lean-to painted bright blue, does not make us want to crawl into bed and stay there. But the dirty old Santas, winter Afternoons, oppress us like the Heft of cathedral Tunes.

The heavy weight of it all! We already owe money everywhere. Our quarterly tax payments to the IRS are due on money we scrounged last summer pushing wheelbarrows full of mulch up the grassy slopes of rich people's houses. We are in debt to the company which insures our rustbucket car, to the utilities which grudgingly supply our light and heat and hot water and telephone. To the town, which is fond of reminding us that living indoors is the shakiest of privileges. We have no firewood. There should be four cords of red-heart oak, nicely split and stacked, drying in the shed. There should be orange juice and hamburger in the freezer, and packages of white fish fillets wrapped in white paper tied with white string. There should be a shelf in the pantry crowded with toilet paper and toothpaste and laundry soap—all those things which food stamps do not buy. When the darkness closes in and the money runs short we are forced to wash our brittle dry hair with bar soap because there is no shampoo. And what if we lose a filling? What happens if we can't start the car one morning? Or can't start the car one night, leaving the wet parking lot of the factory where we've found a couple of months' work stitching logos on hats, for sale before the Super Bowl?

And here comes Christmas. When even the poor relations must have gifts to distribute. No one expects much from us— a couple of jars of summer pickles or some dried herb sachets from the garden. But we are sorry to be underprepared. All those months which were not Christmas, and should have been spent braiding little rugs. Or stitching up an armada of patchwork quilts.

I have heard it said that there is no shame in being poor but that it is damned inconvenient. Yes, and labor-intensive and exquisitely painful each December, when hard decisions must be made. Shall we bake rafts of Christmas cookies to give away? Apparently we are good at making cookies; we appear to have patience for the ridiculously fussy process.

But: where does the butter come from? It comes from our little monthly allotment of food stamps, and will come home with us instead of something else—broccoli, perhaps. The baking chocolate and the Marshmallow Fluff and the real vanilla extract for the pans of fudge will take the place of frozen peas or cottage cheese. The unconscionably expensive walnuts will be made possible by the absence of coffee.

Which has no nutritive value, we remind ourselves. Nothing in it but heat and caffeine. Easily done without. We will trade coffee's transitory pleasure for the ability to hand out wheels of shortbread shaped like the sun. For the opportunity to bake loaves of braided sweetbread. Pans of Parker House rolls, dusted with poppy seeds, as light and good as our intentions.

Oh! We feel our hearts relax! There is nothing in the house for supper but tea and toast, but there are cookies everywhere and even the cold front bedroom at the far end of the house smells of baking. Have we been shaken awake?

And in this way Christmas comes to us, arriving late but intact. On the morning of the twenty-third we go downtown to the post office and rummage through the wire wastebasket for catalogs from Crate and Barrel. We come home and cut out pictures of expensive blown-glass ornaments from Poland and tape them to the gifts which we have wrapped in paper grocery bags. We cut out pictures of Great Danes wearing antlers if that is what the art director pitched this year. We cut out pictures of napkin rings. And dining room chairs. We decorate our gifts with pictures of other people's presents, and then we tie them up with purple yarn.

Strangely, every Christmas Eve we are lashed with the hard warm rain of a coastal storm. Often it will snow for an hour or two in the morning, and the people who moved here by mistake will be relieved to see that things here cannot be so different from what they remember back in the city. We, however, know that by four o'clock, when grocery clerks and store cashiers and people who pump gas would like to be going home, the streets will be full of melted slush. That by the time the doors of retail are locked, and those of us who have been blessed with work rush home to shower and change, the pavement will be black and shiny in the headlights.

And so comes Christmas. We load the backseat of the car with presents, and hustle off. We bring a couple of the broken cookies to eat on the way to church. We park on the street, under one of the raggedy Santas who are being thrown and tossed by the rain, and who nevertheless hold their arms bravely up in seasonal greeting. *Ho! Ho! Ho!* The new people are grievously disappointed by the bare streets and scoured lawns. They want their Christmas white, not wet.

But we are weepy with nostalgia and relief. We laugh and shake the water off our raincoats inside the open sanctuary door. Someone hands us a candle which has been poked into a paper cuff. We find a damp pew and settle in to wait for the shaky processional. We check to make sure that Jesus is still a naked plastic baby doll wired onto some greenery high over the altar. Everything one cares about here must be kept well above the waterline.

The Light Of The World is passed from candle to candle. We sing "Oh Little Town of Bethlehem," and "Away in a Manger"—of all the magnificent hymns of Christmas we sing the most babyish and bland. We are told to Go Forth Rejoicing. Then we are told to blow out our candles and hand them over at the door.

What harm would we do with a lit candle in such a rainy darkness?

In any event, we have our deliveries to make, at houses where we will be welcomed and given rivers of hot coffee and maybe—if the traps were full all summer—some lobster bisque. And if not, then quahog chowder. We will be asked to spend the night, to bless the house by sleeping on the sofa like a traveling prophet. Except that we are honored even here in our own hometown.

Eventually we drift off, sated, promising ourselves that next year we will remember ahead of time how it turns out: warm and dry and washed clean of pain. We will remember that each Christmas we listen to rain falling hard against the roof and the blind windows, in the company of others who do not think of us as poor relations. Who love us. And who are incapable of making us feel at all diminished by our circumstances, and certainly not unwanted.

A Story from the Gospel of Luke

ONCE UPON A TIME, Congress passed welfare reform, and signed it into law.

Even in the Commonwealth of Massachusetts—which was considered to have a relatively generous level of funding and benefits—it became necessary for the poor to have permanent addresses. Only then could they apply for help from the Department of Transitional Assistance, in the town where they claimed residence.

Joseph was twenty-one years old. As a child he had been diagnosed with moderate special needs, and been awarded SSI. He was, with great difficulty and concentration, making his way toward a degree at the community college in Fall River. On the day that he turned twenty-two, however, his benefits would stop and he would be on his own.

His girlfriend Mary was fourteen. She was pregnant, following a rape by her mother's boyfriend. Joseph, when he found out, had driven back to New Bedford and beat the old man up pretty good.

Then Joseph had put Mary in the car, and taken her to the welfare office downtown, where she filled out the paperwork for food stamps, Medicaid, and Section Eight housing.

A month later she was denied assistance because of her age. In two years, when she turned sixteen, she would be able to petition the court to be made an emancipated minor. At which point she could reapply for benefits. In the meantime, she was to be returned to her mother, unless the Department of Social Services put her in foster care.

But before this could happen her water broke. Joseph—who couldn't figure out what else to do—took her to one of the empty garment factories on Belleville Avenue, where the junkies and runaways live, and made her as comfortable as possible while she screamed and pushed. She gave birth to a little boy, and wrapped him in a sweatshirt, and laid him in a cardboard box.

At the same time, there was a crew of scallopers, out in the bay, working twelve-hour shifts. They were also running cocaine, but that is another story. They were pretty high on weed when a squalling, barking horde of seagulls appeared, circling the boat, screeching and flapping and darkening the moon. The crew was afraid. They were *very* afraid. They started to believe that they could hear the birds giving orders, telling them to get back to New Bedford, to look for a child who was destined to save their sorry butts.

At the same time, three professors from UMass Dartmouth—two sociologists and a particularly kind-hearted member of the physics department—were conducting a survey of the city's homeless. They started the night in Weld Square, and moved east toward Achusnet Avenue, until they, too, saw seagulls circling the sky near the Portuguese bakery, making an awful racket. Although they were educated men, and thought of themselves as scientists, they were as superstitious as the rest of us, and imagined that an unnaturally large flock of seagulls, so far from the dump, was a sign of some sort. They went to the abandoned garment factory, where they found a baby, wrapped in a sweatshirt, lying in a cardboard box.

And they kneeled down and looked in his tiny face.

And they, and the crew of the scallop boat, and a couple of heroin addicts, and three deinstitutionalized mental patients (who found none of this at all unusual), stood around and looked at this unauthorized, unlucky child who was so new that he was still staring unfocused at the face of God.

A child so recently arrived that he could still speak the

languages of seagulls and dogs and rosebushes. Who still remembered what the errand is we are sent here to do.

They kneeled around the cardboard box, and hoped that this kid would beat the odds. That he'd survive and grow. And be the one to tell us all the things which we once knew but have long since forgotten.

Bad Day

THIS IS WHAT HAPPENS to you if you wind up poor:

One morning you find a small chip on the biting surface of your left front tooth. You wrap the pennies in the penny jar, and take them to the bank. They hand you several dollar bills, which you take to Wal-Mart, where you buy fluoride rinse and a curtain rod.

The curtain rod is something you have needed to put up a barrier between your books and the sunlight from a southern window. Your books are precious things, as are your teeth. The latter, unfortunately, require work which no dentist in town will undertake, because none of them will accept Medicaid. They have all decided that the Commonwealth of Massachusetts does not reimburse them adequately for cleaning the teeth of the working poor.

Oh well. There are other things to worry over—your four bald tires, your next CT scan, the worn-out gasket around the shower stall which lets water run out onto the bathroom floor (regardless of the importance of regular personal hygiene, this cannot be good in the long run for the plywood underneath the plastic tile).

When you finish your errands, and return to your shabby, well-loved house, you see a notice on the door. You hope that FedEx has been and gone, trying to leave some unexpected shipment of necessities while you were out. A crate of grapefruit, maybe, or a new faucet for the sink. Hope springs eternal, even on the bleakest of days. *Especially* on the bleakest of days.

So you shift the plastic bag which holds the fluoride rinse and curtain rod to your other hand, to pull the postcard from between two rows of mossy shingles by the door.

Which is when you suddenly see your life, as if for the first time. You see the futility of entry-level jobs. Of tenacity. Good will. Of faith and decency and patience. You see—all at once—the hubris of love, the hopelessness of invention, of ingenuity, of good cheer; the vain plodding stupidity of stewardship and the conscientious use of floss:

Bad Day

Your property taxes have gone unpaid too long. The post-card in the door is a warrant from the town clerk's office, a notice reminding you—one more time—of the interim nature of your tenancy; here, or any of the places you believed that you could own.

Fishing

I WAS AT THE Salvation Army store on a
bright sunny Saturday morning, and the place was mobbed. I'd
been there since the door opened at nine, flipping through the
racks. There's not much else competing for my time right now.
Saturday mornings at the Army are the high point of my week.

In line behind me at the checkout was a wiry little guy in
a black Harley shirt and a black leather jacket—presumably
secondhand, like everything else the rest of us were wearing. He
had grown an impressive handlebar mustache and long side-
burns. It occurred to me that he might be an out-of-work character actor whose career as a ranchhand on TV westerns was
in a nosedive. If you made your living playing Rusty the Cow-
poke, nowadays it could be a long time between paychecks.

Of course, acting gigs in general are scarce here in

Greater New Bedford. As are positions in any other cattle-related occupations. Jobs of any kind are few and far between, especially in the winter. Which is why so many of us show up every Saturday at the Army.

"Nice out," he said to me suddenly. "I sure don't want to go fishing."

"Me either," I said stupidly, my arms full of five-year-old Perry Ellis linen separates. It hadn't occurred to me yet that he was actually a fisherman. A scalloper, as it turned out.

"Yeah, I'm leaving this afternoon. I'll be gone fifteen, sixteen days."

"Long time," I said, not paying much attention. I was running an inspection on some Brooks Brothers button-downs. "Where do you go?"

"Canada," he told me. There was a pause. I decided to throw the button-downs back. The collars were worn through to the interfacing.

"But they're reopening the Nantucket Shoals. That'll be good. More work. Shorter trips."

"Uh-huh," I said, still too dim-witted and out of practice to understand. He was testing the waters. In other situations, this kind of thing is called a flirtation. But when you're standing in line at the Salvation Army you already have too much information about each other, and no need to pretend you're somebody you're not. All you've got to show off is your optimism and your ingenuity.

"Yup," he said, "there'll be plenty of work for guys like me—I don't do drugs and I'm a straight, regular guy."

I handed the cashier four dollars and fifty cents, and as she filled a plastic bag with my new clothes, I wished this straight, regular guy a safe trip out to Canada and home.

And said that I'd look for him in fifteen, sixteen days.

Bittersweet

I AM OUTDOORS PULLING bittersweet off the trees, afternoons early in this new century. The world's children and babies have, by consensus, been given dominion over the third millennium. But neither I nor the bittersweet notice any difference.

Celastrus scandens is an introduced species which has done too well here in the temperate climate of the Massachusetts coast. It is a tenacious, twisting, energetic climbing vine, whose bright red berries are much beloved by birds, who spread the seed around everywhere, by the usual method. Sometime around the turn of the last century bittersweet enjoyed a brief popularity as a landscape plant. An ornamental novelty.

Since then, it has invaded the woods and cultivated fields, killed off a less aggressive native species, and covered everything which does not move with a heavy network of vines. Ancient purple beech trees die off slowly, smothered by top-growth which grabs the sunlight. Venerable old pines snap under the extra weight, but do not fall.

Meanwhile, in the absence of trees, the bittersweet grows up on itself. It fills the field beside the saltmarsh with what, in winter, look like African termite hills. It climbs telephone poles. It swallows old railroad trestles, deconstructs stone walls. It grows in through the broken windows of abandoned trucks. It snakes up under the cedar shingles on the side of the house, in a lunatic scramble towards the chimney.

We pull bittersweet when the branches are bare, which gives us more leverage against last year's growth. We cut a rope of vine at ground level—it's the diameter of a garden hose after twelve months of undisturbed success. We grab a handhold as far up as possible, and yank hard. All over town, ladies of a certain age are out doing these reverse bungie jumps, struggling to free the strangling, choking chestnuts and arborvitae.

Every winter we go out and fight last year's weedy mayhem, for possession of our two-hundred-year-old maple trees. Eventually the small inheritors will have to learn to do it for themselves.

In addition to everything else demanded of them, they will have to learn to cut away the twisting mounds of someone else's bad idea. To stay with it until it begins to grow dark, and only then come inside, pink-cheeked, smelling of earth.

Finch Nets

ALL THE GERANIUMS WHICH will be fat with bloom four months from now are being shipped out in cardboard crates—hundreds of three-inch cuttings in every box—and all the greenhouses are hiring us back to poke the silly-looking things into flats.

So we report for work in the snowy dark, carrying lunch and a dry pair of socks. Inside, the greenhouse is warm and damp and sweet smelling. And silent, except for the automated sprinklers, and the finches which fly in open ceiling vents when no one is looking.

We'll get laid off sometime in April, after the primroses go to market and the pansies are under control. But in the meantime they'll give us sixty hours of work a week as long as we're willing to keep our mouths shut about overtime pay. And don't ask questions about this year's crop of weary illegals who are driven up from Providence in an unmarked van and dropped off behind one of the equipment sheds.

These crews of exotic men and women do not speak English, which is important to the labor contractors who have recruited them and the growers who employ them. It prevents them from finding out about things like bathroom breaks and the minimum wage. Or the truth about all the chemicals which are passed off as harmless fertilizers.

Imagine miles of wire benches, closely spaced in the vast expanse of greenhouse; each morning we pick up where we left off the night before. We work in pairs, not because they wish us to have company, but because it somehow forces us to maintain a pace which someone daydreaming on their own could not sustain. Hour after hour we push geranium cuttings into pots of soil, five cuttings to a pot, six pots to a flat. It's not heavy labor, exactly, but by midmorning our feet are wet and cold from the sprinkler runoff which accumulates underneath the benches. For some reason we are not allowed to talk at all, so as the day wears on we sink into the isolation of our own thoughts.

By midafternoon our backs are screaming and we are struggling to keep up. It's deep winter and here we are under glass, surrounded by next summer's flowers. But we are also soaked through to the skin, and filthy, praying hard for the day to end.

Finally, when the natural light begins to fade, we sweep up and drag all the empty cardboard boxes out to the snowy Dumpster. Then go back for the wheelbarrow which is heavy with discarded paperwhites and moribund cyclamen and withered ladyferns which have been written off as losses, pulled from their plastic pots when they no longer merit bench space. We tip it all onto the compost pile. Then reach in and grub around for anything with a little life left in it, which we set down on the icy ground. The survival rate for these frost-bitten naked things, once they come to live with us in our cold houses, is almost one hundred percent. Which is a great mystery.

Then, as we are lining up by the back door, the crew chief barks, "Get those damn birds out of here." We have no idea why it is important that these tiny twittering creatures be caught and sent back into the cold, but no one can go home until they are. There is a moment of frozen silence.

Finally some young kid summons up the strength which everyone else has long since used up. He grabs one of the long-handled finch nets; runs up and down the narrow aisles with it, waving frantically while we stand around and watch. If we weren't dead tired we'd be cheering for the birds, who are swooping happily around the heating ducts and the irrigation pipes. Singing. A tiny bird circus.

Which frees us to straggle out at last to the parking lot, retrieving the condemned hothouse flowers we've saved from certain death. The windowless van is waiting. The driver is watching. Although for some of us our suppers and our over-stuffed chairs are only a couple of miles up the road, for others the city of Providence is still an hour and a half away.

Meanwhile, overhead, startled confused finches circle the greenhouse roof, looking for the way back in; mystified by their repeated displacement into the milky lavender dusk.

Staying

W HY? WHY DO YOU stay in that drafty old house, they ask over and over. And over. They are worried about my judgment. They have seen the snow on my kitchen floor when a winter Nor'easter blows through. They know how cold it gets. They know about the way, in the warm months, it tends to rain down the ceiling fixture in my tiny borning room.

"Borning room" is an antique euphemism for the sick room off the parlor, where eighteenth-century babies were born and eighteenth-century old people lay down to die. My borning room is one of the things which keeps me here, in spite of the abysmal condition of the place. It is where I said goodbye to him, then washed and dressed the body which he no longer needed.

A pair of undertaker's assistants sent by Hospice came and zipped him into a plastic body bag. They rolled him out to the back of a station wagon and drove away. The phone rang fifteen minutes later. My down payment on their services was insufficient, they said, and unless I could come up with the rest in cash they would turn around and drive the body back. Deliver him to me, again.

Things like this teach you to stand your ground. To look darkness in the eye and wait until it is the darkness itself which blinks.

So. He is safely buried in the family plot, in an ancient cemetery where almost all the old people I ever loved are buried too. I have a small piece of real estate there myself. We are all next to a stone wall, where we overlook the municipal maintenance sheds. Where we will lie undisturbed together until the Rapture or—a more plausible scenario—until some point in a hopelessly overpopulated future when the town decides it really needs the space for a new fire station or some extra parking.

At which point the disruption of what remains will not matter to us in the slightest. Because in reality we will have been sitting together all this time, here at the kitchen table, shelling peas. We will have been here always. The heaven which is our home is a place which looks remarkably like this one. Except that it has a new bathroom and a new roof and more reliable central heat.

"How can you stay in that drafty ark?" they ask me. Ark, indeed. I stay because I have become the covenant.

And I stay because of the outside chance that I am wrong about all of this. What if he isn't really dead, but merely suffering an inexplicable amnesia? What if the terrible forgetfulness which keeps him somewhere in Idaho, confounded and lost but nevertheless searching for home, someday clears? What if he's working at a humble job and living in a furnished room? What if after the grocery store closes, and the restrooms are clean, and the endcaps are restocked with magazines and hand lotion—after the carriages are wheeled in from the parking lot and stored next to the silent cash registers—he goes home and tries hard to remember me.

What if he is telling some truck driver about our house and our beehives and the window boxes full of pink nasturtiums? Maybe he can't remember my face or name, but knows that he must get here soon. A series of long-haul truckers may be listening to his stories as they crawl across the empty spaces in the middle of the USA.

So, just in case, I wait here for the sound of his key in the lock. Some night it could happen. Nothing is certain. Nothing would surprise me. I might turn and see him standing exhausted in the cold back hall.

This is what you need to keep in mind: reality is an hypothesis, the product of wildly insufficient data. And all narratives are implausible.

Toll House Cookies

I EXPECT THAT IT will not be long now until I am sought out as a likely prospect for somebody's oral history project. My qualifications include the plain bald fact of my birth in one of the years immediately following World War II, and a willingness to talk to fourth-graders who come prepared with tape recorders and a list of innocent questions:

"What was it like when you were in fourth grade?"

"What books did you like to read?"

"Did you have a dog?"

Their questions will have nothing to do with the stories which I will want to tell, of course. And so, in the long tradition of oral history projects, I will annoy and confuse the young field researchers with loopy speeches about unrelated events of importance to me—and possibly to me alone.

I will try my hardest to cooperate. I will tell them what I remember of how scared the grown-ups were during the McCarthy years. I will tell them how the dime store smelled of fish tanks and parakeets and stamp albums.

But then they will be forced to sit politely while I tell them about the Toll House in Whitman, Massachusetts, which opened its doors to travelers on the road from Boston to New Bedford in 1709. And where, in the 1930s, a woman named Ruth Wakefield invented the famous Toll House Cookie. I will make them listen to me, even though the meaning of my stubborn rambling discourse might not be apparent until years later when some graduate student unearths the transcripts and reads through the part where I explain about having lunch at the Toll House in the last years of its existence:

By the late seventies it was the kind of place where elderly bank tellers were given retirement parties in the middle of the day. I was a young bank teller then, divorced with a small child, and sat far down the banquet table from the honoree. Between us were seated the older tellers and the women who sat all day in a room upstairs, sorting checks by hand into numerical sequence. One of the male loan officers—jobs in those days were assigned strictly by gender—had a seat up front; he had been sent to represent the president himself, who was probably back in his office taking a nap.

I don't remember much about the main course, but am inclined to say that we were given a piece of broiled fish, some canned peas, and a baked potato wrapped in tinfoil. The once venerable Toll House had fallen on hard times. The glassware was speckled and shabby. The fact that the beat-up forks, knives, and spoons were real silverplate made me unaccountably sad.

We were given a dish of vanilla ice cream for dessert. There were no cookies.

The Toll House burned to the ground on New Year's Eve in 1984. Someone came in a year or so later and put up one of the ubiquitous franchise joints that serve hamburgers and chicken nuggets from a drive-up window.

As if from the ashes of Guttenberg's workshop had risen a Xerox machine.

Listen, please, oh as-yet-unborn historians! The Toll House was a real place once. I saw it in its senescence, just before the flames. It was doddering and helpless, and the meals it sold were fit only for old bank tellers and those like myself who saw our futures at the far end of the table.

But there was no need to treat with such disrespect the sacred ground upon which chocolate bars were first stirred into cookie dough. And so the world transformed.

Winter Rentals

IN FEBRUARY I DECIDE to believe that the spine of winter has been broken. That spring will surely come. That I should buy a package of tomato seeds, and germinate the ripe sweetness of next summer in little paper cups set on top of my clothes dryer.

All around me on the street, however, are people stuck in winter rentals who cannot share this uncomplicated pleasure. Or the luxury of anticipating the return of sun-washed gardens full of fruits and flowers. Having moved in two weeks after Labor Day, into the empty summer cottages down on the beach, they understand that when the season reopens they will be gone.

It's a precarious life here for us year-rounders, under the best of circumstances. Young families and single mothers are particularly vulnerable to the seasonal displacements which send lots of us into a financial tailspin. Spending the winter someplace temporary, someplace unequipped for the squalls which blow in off the bay, is nobody's first choice. But the rents are cheap. The beach is quiet. And some years it's the only option.

So people pack up and move in. They put homework papers on the refrigerator door and school pictures on top of the TV. They go to work. They come home. What they come home to, of course, is the landlord's old orange plaid sofa, the landlord's coffee table made out of a fake wooden lobster trap, the landlord's tide charts and paint-by-number pictures of full-rigged sailing ships. In short, the landlord's idea of what it is to live beside the sea.

Meanwhile, the Atlantic Ocean turns a milk gray, and ice the strange color of green Fiestaware freezes in the reedy marshes. Ice piles up on the water's edge. Seaweed accumulates at the waterline. Dog-doo and knots of fishing line and the bleached bones of seabirds litter the hard sand.

Inside the uninsulated, drafty little houses there is limited off-season creature comfort. Snow blows in under the front door but does not melt. Kids sleep in unheated bedrooms, and dress for school in the kitchen, standing in front of the open door of an oven set to four-fifty.

They tough it out. They know for sure that it cannot stay so harsh and cold forever. April comes for everyone.

Including, of course, the landlord, who begins to think about putting his boat in the water. He drives down from Worcester or Boston to play a couple of rounds of golf and eat some fish and chips. By then the ice has broken up in the harbor, the crocuses are in bloom in the puddley front yards.

Which gives the people stuck in winter rentals a sick knot in their stomachs. They start to scramble to find relatives or friends who'll take them in for a couple of months, or let them sleep in the camper. The trees swell with buds, the air once again reeks with the mucky smell of mud and marsh. But people in the winter rentals lie awake nights worrying how they'll manage if everyone ends up in a tent at the state park. Or in the car.

They had no reason, back in February, to plant paper cups with marigolds and tomatoes and morning glories. They knew that spring would come. And that without the means to put down roots of their own, its arrival would be a very mixed blessing.

Wendell

MY FRIEND LOUISE SAYS she is buying, so we are out early, slurping down an enormous breakfast of greasy eggs and toast and bacon, to the great amusement of our waitress and the people in the other booths. Who are appalled that two such big girls should be putting away the homefries and cream gravy.

Louise pours another little plastic pack of cream into her coffee, then leans over and tells me that she feels self-conscious when she prays.

She prays???

To whom?

She lights a cigarette, and tells me she prays silently to someone named Wendell, which is inconvenient, since this is also the name of her dead husband's brother.

Wendell, as far as I can tell, is a deity responsible for the good things of this world, the things which Louise loves with distracted devotion and a pure heart: Percocet, fresh swordfish, diamond jewelry, margaritas, cleaning ladies, lease cars, and the rapidly increasing variety of serotonin reuptake inhibitors.

This is the first time I have heard her express a theology of any kind, much less a coherent one. She seems to have developed an elegant belief system which manages to retrieve theurgy from the entanglements, encrustations, and tedium of piety or purity. Wendell can be reached through the usual channels, but his responses are delivered by the UPS man, who leaves cartons of blessings on her back porch several times a week. The rest of the time, Louise is off in the car doing her own shopping. Wendell helps those who help themselves.

Which is not to say that Louise is lacking in generosity. She showers me with underpants and shoes and other odd, somewhat overly personal gifts. She shows up at the house with bags full of wild rice, and truffle oil, and clotted cream. She seldom lets me say no thank you, as if my refusal of such gifts would cause some deep spiritual wound. As if I were attempting to deny the ground of her being.

So I listen to her tentative explanation of First Cause, as she tips a bottle of ketchup over her fried eggs. And then, while I spread a piece of whole wheat toast with a rubbery square of orange marmalade, I think: When did Louise become a theist, praying awkwardly to Wendell? Who apparently answers awkward prayers with catalogs and free delivery and credit cards with breathtaking credit limits. And is independent, as gods go, because he is not interested in any stupid incarnations in the flesh.

Barney

W HEN BARNEY DIED, AFTER the doctors had done what they could, and determined that his passing had been due to natural causes, his caretaker threw him in the freezer and called Ed.

Who drove over the bridge a few weeks later and picked up the body.

Barney had spent a good part of his life at WHOI, the Woods Hole Oceanographic Institution in Woods Hole. In the aquarium, where he was a particular favorite of the staff who looked after him. At some point he had become depressed, and had stopped eating. And, as Ed says, "How are you going to force a ray to eat?"

A Cow Nosed Eagle Ray, specifically; an exotic fish, flat and elegant. His body sat in Ed's freezer for a couple of months, waiting for some slack time in the ceramic fish industry. Eventually Ed made a mold of Barney the Ray, and added him to the new summer line.

Ed has a little shop on the old road to New Bedford. He sells copies of the shiny colorful scup and stripers and flounder which swim around out in the bay. And sweet candy-colored little tropicals who met their deaths in home aquariums. It's hard to get the big fish, though, before they've been gutted and cleaned by fishermen. And so Ed relies on the kindness of a network of people who make their living disposing of deceased museum exhibits.

"I think this is a fair trade-off," Ed tells me. "Barney was dead, but he'll live forever now and be seen by hundreds of people."

And isn't this promise of immortality through art *exactly* the thing upon which so many of us—also destined to go The Way Of All Fish—hang our slippery hopes?

Married In

S HE SAYS TO ME, "The trouble with *them* is they're just like the Irish."

You may fill in for yourself whomever you please— whomever you imagine could have been the object of such an epithet.

She apparently does not know, or doesn't remember, that I married in. That I am the one who weeps when she hears uilleann pipes, the one who calms herself in the dentist's chair with images of fog and bog and sheep.

That in midlife I was welcomed without questions into a family not long removed from a farm in Donaghadee, County Down, whose only concerns about me centered on my long-standing squeamishness about consuming animal flesh. But I was willing to learn to cook the stuff. Happy to boil corned beef. The bliss of unexpected love made me eager to fry up pans of ungodly smelly kippers in the morning to go with the eggs and creeshie bread which make up the canonical Irish breakfast. And in this way was forgiven my weak stomach and odd palate.

Forgiven all my manifest shortcomings, for that matter. The Irish believe themselves to be stiff-necked and stubborn. As evidence of this they will remind you of the centuries of history given over to resentment about their battles lost, which remain for them fresh losses still. And yet they do not hoard up grievances against those of God's creatures with whom they actually live or work. They seemed to keep no tally cards. It was enough that you could make a brave wee cup of tea, then would sit and listen to their stories, and remember what you heard. It didn't matter if the work you did to earn your keep was humble, and involved a wheelbarrow or a dishrag. It only mattered that you were an ordinary sort of person, who could be depended upon to find an extra bed and a blanket for someone who showed up in the middle of the night needing a place to stay. And that you were sensible enough to know that good manners operated on the Rule of Three: as in, (*one*) "Will you stay here with us?"

"No, no."

(*two*) "Are you sure? It's no trouble at all."

"No, no I couldn't trouble you."

(*three*) "Come now, are you sure you won't stay?"

"Well, all right, I'll stop a bit if you're sure it's not too much bother."

So I have become someone who is not afraid to die. Because she knows she will be met in Heaven at the servant's entrance by a smiling gaggle of the Irish dead.

I ask this woman what she means when she says that "the trouble with them is they're just like the Irish," but then I forget to pay attention to her answer. I am busy listening for angel wings and the sound of common English from a Belfast mouth, from which each vowel is separated into syllables that flutter like clean laundry in the wind.

Coyotes

SOMETIMES WHEN I WAKE up drenched in sweat, I hear coyotes singing.

It's mating season for the coyotes, who live in a pack under the puckerbrush, on the far side of a saltmarsh. I, on the other hand, live alone in this falling-down house in a clearing. And am tossed awake by hot flashes which signal the end of my reproductive usefulness.

I've never actually laid eyes on a coyote, although I sometimes find their scat in the grass near the kitchen door. There is nothing to be afraid of. There are rumors of babies snatched from wicker baskets, of children terrorized, of women hanging laundry who have been set upon, their bare legs bloodied. But can any of this be true? It seems more likely that people who believe such things have been seduced by the idea of wildness in the backyard.

Coyotes hunt at night, when we are in our beds. They tip over garbage cans looking for discarded fruit. They feed on elderly housecats whose careless owners have forgotten to lock them indoors.

And in the hour before dawn they sing. Once upon a time I might have been upset to wake in darkness to the noise of mating season, to the same coyote songs they sing all year but which sound more urgent now. More ancient and strange.

But I am at a time of life when my sleep is fragmented by disturbing dreams and the unpleasant sensation of being microwaved. One of my systems is shutting down; the parts which manufactured estrogen are having a big Going Out Of Business Sale. My internal thermostat has begun to fluctuate wildly. Without warning, I find myself suddenly burning with the ludicrous heat of a dying star.

So it comforts me, when I wake all hot and bothered, to hear coyotes keening across the silence. I kick off the oppressive weight of the covers and get up to stand in front of a cold window. To look up past the telephone wires into an empty sky, searching for the moon.

I am in the process of being separated from the lunar floods, from nature red in tooth and claw. A messy business; I should be glad to be done with it.

But it's mating season. And the system which I have

depended upon to regulate longing and desire has not yet reached stasis. I wake up in my narrow bed, drenched with sweat, for no reason or purpose.

Except, of course, to be allowed to hear the sweet wild polyphonic hymns to spring which fill the unmapped hours before morning.

Scavengers

THE SCAVENGERS ARE BUSY. Retreating glaciers of roadside snow have left a winter's worth of debris exposed. Everywhere you look, beer cans and McDonald's boxes rise out of the sand like Easter eggs, and we go out and collect them.

My own front yard is full of candy wrappers and scratch tickets from the state lottery, paper cups, broken sunglasses. And the occasional baby diaper, which, having been advertised as disposable, was disposed of out the window of a car on someone's way home from the beach.

There is broken glass which must be gathered early, before it disappears beneath new growth of grass and brambles. Otherwise I find it later with my rackety old lawnmower, which makes the process of mowing more dangerous and exciting than it needs to be.

Some of us go out dragging garbage bags and walk the roadsides looking for trash. We do this because we want the place to look nice, and because a stroll up one side of the street and down the other is a pleasant way to spend a sunny afternoon.

Some of us go out to look for empties, which are worth five cents at the redemption center downtown. Even if they have been driven over and are as flat as aluminum matzos. At this time of year a full garbage bag of discarded empties represents about five miles overland. But earns you enough for a quarter-tank of gas, or a pack of cigarettes, if that is your wont.

I do not believe that our circumstances or our professions are chosen for us by our DNA. Nevertheless, the name which my grandfather carried when he arrived here from Russia at the turn of the last century means "scavenger." Like the English surnames Weaver, Farmer, and Smith, it was an occupational title, an inherited one. I was told that coming through the port of Providence, Rhode Island, he decided to choose a new name—something less humble and more American sounding. He picked "Wasserman." In this way I became Wasserman, too, instead of the Russian word for "Dumpster diver."

I believe that once we *all* were slaves in Egypt. That some of us have been set free. A century after my grandfather's arrival, the most hard-pressed still spend the day walking into town with garbage bags thrown over their backs. Walking slowly, stopping every ten or fifteen feet to root around.

But here in our shabby new Jerusalem, no one thinks themselves above those who collect empties to earn a couple of bucks. We know the difference between a pleasant walk up the street and back, performing some mild act of public service, and a long visible trek into town dragging a garbage bag full of cruddy bottles and cans. In good times and lean here, if you are one of the lucky ones in current possession of a car, it is a simple matter of local habit to stop and pick up someone on their weary trip home from town. And of routine decency not to mention, ever, that you saw them on their way in.

Staying Home

GOOD FRIDAY. WHEN EVEN the most apostate among us craves the reassurance of home. Desperately, between the hours of noon and three, when—year after inexplicable year—a thick bank of low clouds rolls across the weak sunshine of eleven o'clock. And sends us on a hunt for our skepticism, thinking it might be a good time to bring it out of storage and check it for wear. Down on Main Street, in late morning, there is a small flurry of nervous activity. Everyone needs to cash a check or run into the Post Office for stamps. To finish up their business and get home. Before the sky darkens.

How is this possible? How can our mythology control the weather on a specific afternoon, on a calendar we long ago considered, and renounced, and believed forgotten?

I am years out now, far from the shore upon which I was washed, stunned and stupid, one Good Friday following Aubrey's death. When I was notified of possible trouble. Familiar trouble. I hadn't realized how common it is for the bereaved to find that they have somehow internalized what they have seen.

How ridiculous it seems at first, to those of us who have already been left behind, to learn that lightning may very easily strike twice. That there are no laws against unequal distribution of certain kinds of unpleasant surprise.

So while we wait the interval required to confirm the diagnosis, or be granted a reprieve, we think about what we have left undone.

Meanwhile our friends, who love us, assume what we will wish to do is travel.

The idea of it, when one may soon be leaving permanently, seemed then, as it seems to me now, the most ludicrous of all responses to a bad biopsy report. I was, on that Good Friday, already so far from home, in the land of magnetic resonance imaging and endocrine panels. It was terrain which I had been forced to memorize earlier, during Aubrey's final illness. I was familiar with its awful smells and hard upholstered waiting room chairs and the temporal displacement of patients who have been triple-booked and told to sit quietly in exquisitely uncomfortable chairs while great painful mysteries are discussed behind closed doors.

So when it seemed my turn had come to be the patient,

rather than the patient's terrified advocate, I was immediately homesick. Why would I want to spend what useful time remained to me in some motel room, sleeping on an unfamiliar, common mattress, the light of some strange morning held back by musty rubber-backed drapes, pulled across a window which looked out on the parking lot?

Why would I want to wash the body which I was told I would soon vacate in some blank motel shower, and having dressed in folded clothing hauled with me from home, walk down dank carpeted hallways to the elevator? And go to some disconsolate function room, where breakfast would be waiting in stainless steel warming tanks; where I might choose a ladleful of scrambled eggs, or a Danish pastry, and a carelessly assembled portion of fruit salad—someone else's cantaloupe, someone else's purple grapes, someone else's grapefruit segments, sweetened with corn syrup from a gallon bucket in the motel kitchen. Choosing, then, to carry the thick white plate of breakfast buffet to a waiting table, where someone would come and turn my coffee cup right side up and ask did I prefer regular or decaf?

But why?

All I wanted then—and all I continue to want, now that I am safely back among the living—is the comfort of my own bed and my own chair. And my own blue-flowered dishes.

Is this odd? To have an unforgiving preference for evenings in front of a good friend's fireplace to ones stuck in a smoky booth, looking at a bowl of iceberg lettuce and a few pale tomatoes, waiting for a pizza, and coloring on the place-mat with stubby crayons from a paper cup next to the red pepper flakes?

Is it stubborn to believe that those things which are essential for the maintenance of life are best when they are clean of commerce? And are not products of the minimum wage, or worse?

Homemade clothing, for example. Even if the button-holes are not perfectly spaced. Homemade curtains, and homemade pillows to sit on freshly vacuumed parlor chairs. Why should I apologize for my noisy preference for what is sacred, when our gross national product might easily be used as a measure of the profane? I know the difference between a loaf of bread made in one's own unreliable oven and bread which is made by day labor; the day labor must spend a long tired shift far from home, confined indoors and wishing for the comfort of supper and bed.

Ask me how I know these things.

If you should find yourself one day, sitting with your keys in your hand in the front seat of your car, parked outside a clinic which treats tumors, say, or something else—MS, per-haps, or Huntington's—dumbstruck by the news of your impending cancellation, would you want the consolation of exile? Would you ask to be sent to visit Yellowstone? Beijing? Provence?

Or would you want to get home quickly, and make yourself a cup of cocoa, and sit in clean pajamas while you watched the lights go on in all the houses up and down the street? Wouldn't you prefer to know that you were safe inside the only place which you had called forth into being—the only place on earth which held your books and all your photographs and which was so familiar that you might walk it blind.

The only place whose whitewashed walls depended upon you for their continued existence. The only place which remembered all that you had done, and been, and been asked to do without.

Burning Brush

A DAY AFTER RECEIVING the nasty but strangely routine phone call about a suspicious shadow on an x-ray film, I noticed something unexpected about my behavior: that while mortality should have been old news, I was nevertheless acting like it was the first time I'd seen the memo.

Time stopped, and I moved into a dimensionless world of distracted self-absorption. I'd been showing up for routine equipment maintenance at the clinic downtown, just like everyone else, on the conscientious schedule prescribed for grownups. There's not much to it. You know the drill. You take a couple of deep breaths. You hold out an arm for a blood draw. Then you step on the scale. It is only the latter of these little procedures which causes me the slightest discomfort. I leave the office feeling relieved and silly.

So the old enemy's possible acquisition of a prime piece of my personal real estate was an unexpected bit of business. A strange stillness settled over me as I waited for further results. And so, to test the limits of my courage and my character, I went out into the windless morning to burn brush.

Every winter I prune away the deadwood in the yard. I tread the snowy ground, retrieving silver maple branches that have broken in the wind. I collect pine cones that have fallen in the driveway. I throw everything onto a pile in the clearing behind the house.

And later I clean the flowerbeds. I rake up the woody stems of last year's perennials and throw them on the pile. I pull the dried-up iris blades off this year's corms. And on a still day near the equinox, when light and darkness are once again in balance, I go down to the fire department and get a permit to burn.

That year, as always, I came home from town and got two rakes out of the shed. I got my wheelbarrow and an old metal chair. I brought out the hose for the first time since fall, then went down into the dark, cobwebby dirt-floored cellar and opened the outside valve. I tidied the brush pile, positioned the hose, pulled on heavy leather gloves.

And then I lit the match.

Flames leapt twenty feet into the air, high and hot and noisy. It was calm midday, the sun was shining for the first time in months. I felt the fire against my face, and watched grapevines and hollyhocks and stringy little balls of clematis become heat and light. And soft gray ash.

After a while I grew bored and restless, and was relieved when three o'clock came and I was required by the terms of my burn permit to turn a hose on the smoking remains.

The next day I went back out to shovel up the charcoal and grit. And spread it on my compost pile.

It was an act of faith, which sometimes looks very much like plain bald defiance.

Demons

I

T HAS RAINED FOR weeks. It will rain for-
ever. Nothing will ever change. We will grow spongy in the
damp, and after our houses are consumed by rot and weather,
we ourselves shall wake one morning punky and rotten.

There are thunderstorms every night. Lightning strikes old
trees, which might burn like piney torches at some other time
of year. But in the season of downpour they merely spark and
fizzle. We call the fire department anyway. They tell us that
someone will be over right away to look at things, but we hear
annoyance in the dispatcher's voice. Can't a foolish woman see
that the rain will douse the sparks, that no harm will come to
her or to her soggy house? He is right, of course, and eventually someone with a red light on the dashboard of their pickup

truck drives by the place, slowly, and off down the street into the night.

Meanwhile, mice and squirrels run the floorboards overhead. If it isn't one thing, it's another. Deluge and darkness and the threat of immolation—and at the same time the sound of creatures scuttling and chewing behind the ancient horsehair plaster.

One year, I spent a demon-ridden winter listening to the domestic lives of raccoons who had climbed down one of the chimney flues in late fall, and taken up residence in my beehive oven. I was unprepared for the ferocity and discord of the species.

Most people know enough not to throw animal flesh onto the compost pile. Not because eggshells or moldy casseroles would do any harm. But we know that carnivores are as covetous of our real estate and our peace of mind as they are of our garbage. Skunks, drawn by ill-considered recycling programs involving high-protein leftovers, will eventually climb in one of the rotted cellar windows, and take up residence in the dank recess underneath the kitchen. Wild dogs, made mean and feral by their abandonment at the end of summer by people headed back to the city, will snarl at us from hiding places underneath the porch, will breed and begin to run in packs, and then—according to local logic—will become aggressive and ambitious. So that someday when we are carrying bags of groceries into the house we will be surounded and attacked.

A pack of hungry mongrels with yellow eyes will nip at our arms. And then, while we are disoriented and immobilized by fear, they will rip apart the cartons of milk and juice and the packages of cheese strewn across the lawn.

But it is unnecessary to have firsthand experience of such fully imagined terrors to be convinced that there are dark forces, and that they operate through the agency of neighborhood wildlife.

If it has rained for weeks, and all the iris bulbs you planted in hope and haste one bright day back in early March have long since rotted in the cold, and if you are forced to listen in the darkness to the lightning storms which travel nightly up the watery alley of Canal, out at the far end of the marsh, it is easy to believe that the snarling and screaming of raccoons behind the thin metal door of the bake oven are the announcement of your damnation.

That the manic confrontations in the ceiling, which is only fiberboard and dry as papyrus, are more than simply squirrels settling their squirrely arguments about hierarchy dominance. You are being persecuted by nature itself, which resents your life indoors.

It wants to rot the cornerboards and dissolve the sills. It wants to strike the roof peak with lightning, and send you out barefoot into the wet night. It sends squirrels to chew through the antique wiring. Chipmunks to shred your clothes and papers in boxes in the attic. It causes mice to die in the walls, where they putrefy and stink, a smell familiar to inhabitants of old houses, which is best described as dirty diapers mixed with wildness and fur.

It resents your walls and your storm doors. It does not want you to sleep deep and heedless in some secure bed.

Which is how you find yourself climbing the stairs with a box of mothballs in your hand. "It is a violation of Federal Law to use this product in a manner inconsistent with its labeling. NOT FOR USE TO CONTROL SQUIRRELS, BATS AND BIRDS IN THE HOME."

You pour the poisonous pleasant-smelling benzene derivatives down a knothole in the floorboards, and behind the door of the glory hole underneath the pitch of the old roof. You throw some behind the beehive oven.

The next day the house is quiet. The unheated upstairs bedroom smells heavily of mothballs, but there is no longer anyone at home who sleeps there. You are a felon, with a spare room full of toxic fumes. But because you are old enough to remember when the world was an orderly place which routinely smelled of naphthalene, you feel nostalgic rather than guilty.

And in this way you find strength enough—at last—to wait out a few more weeks of drizzle and cold, inside the shelter of a freshly silent house.

Sea Glass

I WAS STARTLED TO see the wet sand covered with something that looked exactly like silicone breast implants. Which I realized, after a minute or two, were just jellyfish. But exotic ones, blown in by an unseasonable shift in the Gulf Stream.

I'd gone to walk the beach at midtide, at midday, looking for sea glass before the summer people arrived, while the place was still deserted and wild. And full of broken shells and wormy broken two-by-fours and odd pieces of weather-beaten plastic flotsam. Before tourists cleaned the beach of any sea glass and left behind a thousand cigarette butts sticking out of the sand, like stubble in a field.

Everybody here once had a peanut butter jar full of sea glass they'd collected over time. Pieces of colored glass ground smooth and opaque by the action of the tides lined the windowsills of every cottage. They were pressed into the wet concrete of birdbaths and retaining walls. Were sent home in the pockets of visiting children.

It was everywhere, as common a find as the flat translucent orangey shells called "sailor's toenails" which are responsible for my lifelong aversion to sailors. But because sea glass was the product of bottles tossed overboard, and garbage dumped a few miles offshore, its disappearance is one of the unintended consequences of the massive decade-long cleanup of the bay. The subsequent proliferation of sailor's toenails, of course, is another.

All the broken glass, there in the mucky flats at low tide, when the sea pulls away and lets us see what's underneath, had been rendered harmless. It was delivered to us in pieces no bigger than a nickel. Rough edges gone. Soft bits of blue and green and brown and creamy white. Sometimes the rare prize piece of inexplicable lavender or red.

We'd walk the beach at low tide, looking at our feet. Go home with a handful of sea glass, as if we were accumulating tiny tokens of affection from the wide, churning Atlantic Ocean, roiling up the bay.

Now that offshore dumping has been outlawed, and everyone understands that throwing garbage overboard is a shameful thing to do, sea glass seldom washes in with the clamshells and the sailor's toenails.

But now—inevitably—you can *buy* sea glass which has been manufactured from bottles which are smashed and artificially weathered to look like actual debris.

It's packaged and sold in little plastic bags. Some of which, when empty, find their way into the stomachs of sea turtles who mistake them for our familiar native jellyfish—a tragic consequence which was certainly unintended, but which cannot have been unexpected by anyone who'd seen the public beach in July. When it looks like a drought-stricken acre of Marlboros that's been seeded over with a cover crop of Styrofoam cups and candy wrappers and Ziploc baggies half full of abandoned ham sandwiches.

Although the sea is vast and powerful, its ability to take our garbage and transform it into treasure cannot keep pace with our ability think up new varieties of witless trash. New ways to foul the water and poison the shore.

So it retaliates, apparently, by sending us hapless tropical jellyfish, who have been caught by a temporary freakish shift in the Gulf Stream and carried north, far beyond where they belong. It flings them on the beach. And watches us as we encounter what must be a shipwrecked load of prosthetic devices, brought in on a single tide.

And laughs at us, at the shiver of fear and recognition. At the momentary vertigo we feel seeing all those breast implants piled up, like warning shots across our bow.

The Herring Run

MY HERRING PERMIT IS good for almost another month, but the truth of it is that the herring themselves will stop running in a week or so. They swim up from Florida, and come back to spawn in the freshwater ponds and rivers where they somehow remember spending their fishy childhoods.

The process became almost impossibly complicated for them about two hundred years ago, when dams were built everywhere, to harness the running water which powered the Industrial Revolution here in New England. The herring could not make it past the man-made obstructions without help, and so Colonial legislatures and local government got into the business of mandating fish ladders and catch limits, so that everyone would have a fair share of the millions of silvery things that swim in from the ocean in the early bright days of spring.

Few of us still make pickled herring, a simple procedure involving vinegar and a brick. Most of the herring permits are sold to people who use the fish for bait to catch other bigger fish. This seems silly to me, but who am I to argue. Squanto, you will remember, showed the new people in town how to increase crop yields with a herring in each hill of corn. I am not such a purist, but I do enjoy the sight of a freezer full of pickled herring, waiting to become part of a winter supper.

So I drive out to our Herring Run, which is located on a disconsolate strip of highway between two defunct and crumbling red brick factories, next to the Elks Hall. A sign says, "Agawam Herring Run—In Operation Since 1632." My guess is that this is off by about three or four thousand years, but that date may refer to when the squabbling started.

I get my drywall bucket out of the car, and line up in front of the herring shed, waiting for my portion of the catch. The sound of water roaring through the culvert under the highway almost drowns out the sounds of traffic headed for the Cape. In front of me in line are a couple of guys who have driven up from New Jersey to do some fishing and some drinking; not necessarily in that order. They did not think to buy a permit at Town Hall. Twenty bucketsful for twenty dollars, ten buckets for ten, scooped up out of the run by the Herring Agent, and handed over by him to the permit holders at the rate of one bucket per day per customer. The Herring Agent, an older gentleman, a Swamp Yankee of great patience and few words, explains to them why it is not possible for him to let them have four or five unauthorized pails of fish, even if they slip him a couple of bucks for his trouble.

"God *damn* it!" they say, making sure the rest of us can hear. "We drove all the way up here to go fishing, and the bait store's closed. Don't you know it's our money that keeps your economy going? We're the ones who keep you people alive." They curse a few more times, and then repack the coolers and cartons of beer and the rubber waders they'd spread out on the tailgate of their pickup.

After they've gone, and I'm on deck, waiting for the young assistant to empty a net full of squirming bluebacks into my drywall bucket, the Herring Agent laughs and says, "Hell, the only money they're spending around here is at the package store and the bars. And they ain't even staying here—they're at a motel over on the Cape!"

So I am home now, monitoring the pickling process of fish which had felt compelled to come back to town. It has been explained to me by a load of tourists why and in what ways we locals are low on the food chain, but I can't for the life of me figure out what advantage accrues to using little fish to catch bigger fish, if all you wanted in the first place was a cold beer and a night at some motel over the Bridge.

New Gardens

U<small>P AND DOWN THE</small> street, all over town, people are out digging around as if they know what they're doing. Little pots of flowers are being plunked down everywhere, and I cringe to see the poor leafy things, strangling in newly dug beds. Doomed by the enthusiasm and reading habits of people who believe that flowers are installed, like carpeting. And are made of the same uncomplaining stuff.

I blame magazines for giving people the idea that every house should look like it is lived in by some cheerful, demented Victorian spinster. Grocery store magazines, the ones on the racks beside the checkouts, are full of lurid photographs of tuberous begonias in full display behind some beautifully restored shingle-style bungalow. Of close-up shots of coneflowers and blue salvia and edible pink daylilies spilling from raised beds framed by real cobblestones, the kind that arrived here as ballast in the cargo hold of some long-ago sailing ship.

Photographs of striped heirloom tomatoes, growing up the wall of a darling garden shed, where the owners keep their collection of nineteenth-century watering cans and English rubber boots.

None of these images bear the slightest relationship to the realities of normal people's lives. We do not have grounds-keepers, landscape architects, or even someone to explain to a beginner what "soil pH" means or why it matters. The yards around here are mostly sand, anyway, so near the ocean, and few of us can afford to have someone dump a load of good dark topsoil where we plan to put the petunias.

But people are beguiled by the magazine dreams of ferny glens and deep, scented bowers, where life is sweet and easy and will bloom continuously until some distant hard frost.

The truth of it, of course, at least for the people I know, who put a row of shade-loving hostas in a straight line out by the sun-baked street, and then some straggly, stunted little marigolds—which crave full sun—under the overhang of their saggy decks, is that flowers are as vulnerable as we are to the vicissitudes of climate and chance.

That the proportion of darkness and light makes a great deal of difference, in the lives of men *and* moonbeam coreopsis. That beyond the need to be fed and gently treated, it is crucial that you had the good fortune at some point in the past to avoid being planted where you didn't belong.

Memorial Day

FOR A MONTH NOW all the Boston TV stations have been showing us pictures of college students rollerblading along the Charles River in what purports to be sunshine. We have no way of knowing whether these are documentary films; the low gray horizon here makes us suspicious.

But with any luck the sun will finally come out for good the week before Memorial Day, and we will decide that All Is Forgiven. This place is like a bad boyfriend who has scowled at us through too many crummy restaurant dinners. All winter he has been a glowering, gloomy presence, expecting us to be made compliant if not happy by the occasional plate of baked schrod, and we have been at a loss to explain his continued presence in our lives.

But the week before Memorial Day the sun comes out,

and everything is green and tender and we are in love. Foolishly. As if there is any other kind of love.

The place reeks of lilacs, around all the old houses which have not yet changed hands. When new owners come in they will uproot the bushes which droop under deep lavender panicles in May, because these people won't arrive until July, after school lets out. By then the lilacs are covered with powdery mildew, which thrives in the damp sea air and causes the leaves to curl strangely at the margins. In addition, the undisciplined growth habit of the species, which is so charming in spring, alarms the new people. Who will also shear their forsythia bushes into blocky submission, believing them to be no different from the city hedges with which they are familiar.

And the beach plums are in flower! Little wild plum bushes, gnarled and inconspicuous the rest of the year, blooming in the sandy scrub beside the road and all along the interstate, where they find the harshness and inaccessibility which they need to prosper. The fruit is much prized by gatherers who grew up believing what Euell Gibbons wrote about the superiority of undomesticated forage. These people are, for the most part, unaware of the toxins which accumulate in plants which grow beside a highway. They will park beside the median strip on a hot day later in the summer, and take their basket-carrying lives in their hands, standing in front of beach plums which are growing within six feet of the gasoline trucks and freight haulers, bound for Canada or New York City.

When I pick beach plums I go into the field beside the marsh, or drive out into the woods where I know there will be unadulterated little stands of plum. I'm seldom ahead of the deer, who love the sour purple things. And beach plums are not prolific bearers; they are fussy about the weather during the weeks when they set fruit. So even in a good year I am unlikely to come home with enough to make much of a batch of jelly. Two or three small jars at most.

So where does all the beach plum jelly come from? It is as iconic here as lobsters and lighthouses. It even sits on the counter at the video store. Everyone sells little jars of jelly the color of very good amethysts, capped with a circle of lavender gingham and a label which says "Product of Cape Cod." Is there a secret beach plum forest on an undiscovered, unmapped invisible offshore atoll? The bushes resist cultivation. They hate to be moved. There are no beach plum farms or beach plum cooperatives or beach plum consortiums. I have never heard rumors about smuggling operations, where crates of little wild fruits are being off-loaded from ships whose cargo manifests show them to have originated in Hong Kong.

In any event, when the beach plums flower, the air is so sweet and heavy with the scent of bloom that you try hard to remember if there is something which they remind you of, but have forgotten.

Which is why we have Memorial Day.

When we may wear white without feeling ignorant. And

can finally put the tender annuals in the ground. Memorial Day weekend is the official opening of the yard sale season. It is also, for better or worse, when the summer people arrive to open up their cottages.

Meanwhile, those few of us who have the day off from work march down Main Street. To remember is a duty, and we are pleased to do the heavy lifting. The summer people do not participate. They are too busy airing out their mattresses and making sure the refrigerator still works. They are unpacking cartons of groceries brought from home, certain that the local A&P has a secret two-tier pricing system meant to bleed them dry.

We assemble at the harbor downtown, where someone from the VFW gives a speech about patriotism and duty. The tourists pay no attention as they drive by. Someone helps an elderly veteran in a wheelchair to the edge of the town dock, where he throws a wreath of acanthus leaves into the water, in memory of those lost at sea. We weep a little. If the tide is coming in, the wreath refuses to float out and away, and instead gets trapped under the pilings of the pier where we are standing.

We all pretend not to notice.

Then the town cops line the cruisers up and close off all of Main Street—to the consternation of the tourists who forgot about the parade, and are trapped in their cars while they watch us troop by. The high school band plays "America the

Beautiful" over and over; it is a mercifully short distance to the Green. Even so, the oldest veterans begin to look pooped by the time they get as far as the Post Office, and we are all suffering in the heat.

But the kids in the middle school marching band have little trouble keeping up the pace. They too have only one song in their repertoire. It takes us about ten minutes to figure out what the heck it is—they are playing a wildly and endearingly fragmented version of "I Heard It Through the Grapevine."

Oh and I'm just about to lose my mind.
Honey, honey yeah.

A moment of silence is called for when we reach our destination on the Town Green. A tiny girl steps forward to lay flowers on the Civil War Memorial, at the feet of a grand granite seaman who is standing an unending watch, searching the long-ago horizon through blind granite binoculars.

Then we disperse, and the cops start waving carloads of hot grumpy summer people out into traffic. They are thinking how grateful they are that the damn parade is over.

We who are wrapped in the heavy scent of beach plums are thinking about how grateful we are for the numberless sacrifices which were made in order that little kids could grow up safe here, playing fractured Motown oldies on borrowed trombones.

And some of us are also grateful to be reminded one more time of the fragile overwhelming sweetness of this place.

Side Chairs

W

HAT WILL REMAIN, ACCORDING to our scientists, after humans are extinct, will be a quiet planet writhing with termites. They will survive chemical or nuclear disaster. Epidemics, floods, fire, and war.

They may survive, but they will not be alone. They will share a depopulated earth with an entirely unexpected climax species: old chairs.

I know this because of what I know about side chairs. And the way they multiply in the dark. If you put a little unused Victorian side chair in the attic, and do not return to check on it until next spring, you will then find *three* side chairs, sitting in the musty stillness, innocent as kittens. Years later, your children, going about the somber business of cleaning up your effects after you have been promoted to glory, will climb the stairs to find a set of *twelve* chairs, their brittle cane seats covered with fly specks and rodent droppings. "I don't remember these," your children will say. "Where did Mother get an entire set of dining room chairs, and why did she keep them in the attic?"

The eerie metaphysics of furniture is even more obvious at the dump, where its ability to manipulate our behavior is out in the open for anyone to see. I submit for your approval, as Rod Serling used to say, the example of two Saturdays ago. A fine bright dry day, the world as full of promise as a row of peas. I dressed carefully. Put on some lipstick. And headed off.

I had nothing to dispose of. I suffer from the sort of prideful compulsive tidiness common to those of us who are always broke, but believe our ship is coming in. I prefer bare swept floors to shabby carpet, an empty back hall to one filled with rusty clam baskets and broken oars. But I do enjoy a little harmless conversation with the guys in pickup trucks who come to crawl around, looking for parts. There is always a large assortment of these men at the dump on Saturday morning.

And a large assortment of chairs. Rump-sprung aluminum beach chairs. Old metal motel chairs. Lawn chairs and porch chairs and gliders. Highchairs. Office chairs. Folding chairs. Bar stools. All of them doomed to be squashed by the bulldozer at closing time. Including, that day, a set of six old soda-fountain chairs in good condition. For which I had not the slightest use.

"Want me to put those in your trunk for you?" he asked, a lovely gray-haired man about my age. Clean pressed shirt. Work-roughened hands. Dark eyes and no wedding ring. And no shadow where one had recently come off.

So into the car they went, these chairs I did not want. And into the woodshed, where they now are safe from rain and ruin. Six more antique chairs which will survive past the Day of Judgment because—as certain other social pathogens which destroy one's sanity might have done—they used me and my instinctive weakness for kind men with pickup trucks.

Six more chairs which will quietly multiply and grow in number until someday they inherit an empty world, with lots of places to sit down.

Men and Geese

A LADY IN MIDDLE age finds herself kneeling in front of her herb garden, calculating the percentage of the American population which is of the appropriate gender, age, and availability to become the object of her inchoate romantic longings. And how many of that small number are likely to find her remotely attractive. It is a discouraging math problem.

Not that she wastes a large part of her waking day on such things. She has, after all, a large supply of happy memory to draw upon. One great love per lifetime exceeds what we are guaranteed, even in the Constitution, which merely says that we are free to *look* for happiness. She has been luckier than most, and knows this one true thing, even if it has been years since someone else's body warmth left echoes on the sheets during brief trips to the bathroom at two o'clock in the morning.

But it is just such small remembered pleasures which cause her to imagine what might still be plausible, if not possible.

She goes out into her garden in the afternoon to weed. She pulls the field grass from the tarragon, blade by blade. It is a precision task involving focus and concentration. But it is one of those warm, sleepy days when even a lady in middle age feels the sap rising and wonders what her chances are of ever being asked again by a gentleman if perhaps she would like to sit under his pergola and watch the sailboats on the bay?

The sun grows hot on her face. She hears the honking of geese—it is the next-door neighbors' flock of fat white birds, come waddling over through the puckerbrush to see what she is doing. She notices that the old gander, a saggy-bottomed creature with a loose gray wattle, is looking at her, and she smiles back.

Perhaps it is the eye contact. A second later he is standing in front of her, goosing his neck around in a frank display of arousal.

She tells him gently that he is a beautiful bird. That she is flattered by his attentions. But that she is not interested. And returns her attention to a shaggy clump of English thyme.

Which is when she feels a sudden weight on her back, and sharp claws.

She is shocked. Appalled. She has done nothing to encourage this behavior.

She grabs a bamboo rake and waves it at the gander, who turns his head away and hisses something which she believes means, "Shoot, woman, I can do better than you. I've got a whole *flock* of women following *me* around."

She thinks about this for a while. She thinks that maybe once you got past the webbed feet it wouldn't be so bad. It never is.

A woman in middle age goes out to tend her garden. Buds are swelling on the branches of the lilacs and the sky is a shade of blue that has not been seen all dreary gray winter. She kneels in front of a tender row of spindly flax, and thinks that she might forgive this winged creature his foolishness and misguided enthusiasm. She understands that both of them, two old birds, are simply obeying the imperatives of spring.

And, furthermore, how could he know that it is impossible for man or beast to compete with the memory of a great love lost?

June Weddings

T HERE HAVEN'T BEEN ANY decent manu-
facturing jobs in this town since the end of the American Revolution, when wealthy shipbuilders—who were loyal to the
King—left in a hurry for Nova Scotia. And have not been seen
since.

Now we rely for our survival on jobs in the hospitality
industry. Which for us means tourism and foster care.

Foster care is a huge part of our economy—how crude
this sounds! But there are thousands of kids in the Commonwealth who need someplace to live; who can't or won't go
home. Meanwhile lots of us have an extra bed and some experience raising children. Lots of us have stockpiled more patience than cash. And think that we might have the strength
and character to love a recently arrived stranger, knowing that

they are only passing through on the way to hard-won adulthood.

So for a couple of hundred dollars a month, and extra food stamps if we are already involved with the Department of Transitional Assistance, we become the only family that some of these kids have left. And perhaps they become the same for us.

In any event, the little kids arrive pale and scared, and it takes a while before they loosen up. If they've been in other placements, sometimes it's months before they're secure enough to get themselves a glass of juice from the refrigerator without asking first.

The big kids—the ones on the edge of adolescence— who come from the cities of Brockton or New Bedford, are usually sent into exile here on purpose. The Department wants them to make new friends. Different friends.

And so they do. With any luck we get to keep them long enough that they learn to make a bed and clean a fish and reboot a computer. Long enough to graduate from the high school, which then makes this their official hometown.

Long enough for us to open the mailbox one day and find an invitation to a wedding.

It is a singular honor, to be included in such an event. We show up at the church at two o'clock on a fine bright Saturday in June. Main Street is quiet. There is no problem finding a place to park.

A young usher takes our arm, and escorts us into the darkened old church. "Bride's side or groom's?" he asks. One side of the church is full. The other side is not.

This is—for me—the most sacred moment in the ancient ceremony. This is *our* village, and *our* child, whom we have raised. My chest tightens. And I take a seat on the empty side of the church—always—regardless of my other connections to the members of the wedding party.

They will not stay in town. They can't. They'll leave for jobs elsewhere, or join the Service, in order to have some way to pay for college when they get out.

But before they leave they stand in front of us to begin, in blind faith, the construction of their lives on the modest foundation we provided in exchange for a couple of hundred dollars a month and some extra food stamps.

The Amish

I SPENT A COUPLE of winters stocking shelves overnight at one of a string of cavernous discount gift shops over on the Cape. Loading the freight lift with sixty-pound shipping cartons of silverplated picture frames made in China. And beer glasses made in China. And decorative ceramic bakeware made in China. Someone else got to reload the bins of potholders from China and placemats from China, and paper napkins from China, which was the best gig in the store because paper napkins weigh nowhere near as much as Chinese lasagna pans.

In all my time there, it never once occurred to me to wonder what the Amish would buy in a place like this. I would have assumed—had it occurred to me to think about it—that there would be nothing there the Amish would want. They don't

157

seem to be people who are fond of lawn sprinklers in the shape of fat ladies in bikinis, or of lavender plastic pool toys, or CD compilations of Dean Martin's Greatest Hits.

And what would the Amish actually need? They make their own rugs, for example, so one assumes they wouldn't be interested in the rugs which people in China make. Also by hand. For sweatshop wages, judging from the astonishingly modest prices which the store gets for the truckloads of stuff that go out the door. The Amish wouldn't need jelly or fake sleigh bells or little red-and-white-striped plastic lighthouses made in China.

But in the Hyannis store recently—in the middle of a stolen guilty afternoon of recreational shopping—I found myself next to a couple from Ohio. Who had left their ten children at home, and gone off on a bus tour of Cape Cod. At the suggestion of their oldest son. Who had come to the Cape the year before, and had returned home dazzled, insistent that it was time for his parents to see the world.

And so there they were, doing some shopping. An Amish couple about my age. She in white starched cap and traditional long modest black dress. And black sneakers. He in heavy trousers which I believe she must have made herself from wool which she first spun from sheep which they had sheared.

They had spent the morning looking out the bus window at the Kennedy Compound, and for lunch had eaten lobster. Lobster did not make much of an impression on them, as far as I could tell. They were looking forward to the evening meal, which they had been told would be beef.

So what do the Amish choose to bring back as souvenirs of their visit to the shore? In this case, a pair of baskets which someone in China had painted with cranberries. A little box of cranberry bread mix. And a handful of plastic holly. We spent a long time together looking at a rack of alphabet-bead bracelets, but didn't find the names of anyone they knew.

Before the bus took them away to the steak house, they told me that back in Ohio they are forced to live with a constant stream of visitors who come just to look at them. They thought it would be interesting to see what it feels like to do the looking.

I waved to them as the bus pulled out of the parking lot, their laps full of plastic holly and Chinese baskets and bread mix. Anxiously fixated on red meat and fries as they made their way to Martha's Vineyard.

Little Frieda

WE HAVE NOTICED THAT back where the People Who Moved Here By Mistake come from, the child-centered home is apparently the norm. That the children of the distant upper middle class are relentlessly precious darlings who are encouraged to express their manifest destiny in front of the grown-up company.

That adults are shushed, if we are in midsentence, by parents who are proud to offer us a ground-floor opportunity to get in on the making of the next generation of the American meritocracy.

Sometimes this creates problems.

"Well, yes, I suppose it would be a good idea to involve kids in town government," you are saying in response to some well-reasoned argument for allowing six-year-olds to sit on the Shellfish Advisory Board and the Sewer Commission. You are thinking, of course, that these people are straight crazy and that it will be another hour before you can make a polite getaway.

"More coffee?" they ask. "It's Armenian Roast—you can't get it down here. It's what we miss most about Cambridge."

Oh! Cambridge! Where the streets are scented with unobtainable coffee, opportunities for happiness are as freely distributed as advertising flyers, and children are the little kings and queens of their parents' well-established lives. Where children are, in fact, a midlife career change for people who had always lived on the Red Line, always worked near Harvard Square.

"No thank you," you say, already buzzed on your first helping of the stuff, which tastes as sour and gritty as Portland cement. "So you were telling me about your plans to start a Biodiversity Theater Festival here in July? Workshops? Lectures? Environmental poetry slams? Sounds exciting." You are busy picking cat hair out of the warm blue-corn muffin which is on a plate in front of you. No one seems to notice.

"Yes!" they say. "We have friends who run one in Chicago every year. It's a wonderful experience for everyone. Original theater pieces and open performances for the whole community. It would be great for the town. It would give the kids here something to do."

Other than fish and play in the woods, you mean? Or, in

the case of the ones who are old enough to have cars, work at the A&P stocking shelves to earn money for gas, tires, and a brake job? It occurs to me that I would be required to pass up an unconscionable number of yard sales in order to participate in the Saturday morning sessions of a biodiversity poetry slam.

Meanwhile there is screeching from the direction of the bedrooms in the back of the house.

"Oh good! Frieda is awake! We were afraid you would miss your first chance to meet her. She doesn't usually sleep past five, but when we told her last night that you were coming, she got busy collecting things to show you, and was up quite late."

And out comes little Frieda, in a rumpled nightgown and the cowboy boots which she has worn to bed. A darling child I guess will go to first grade in the fall. She has a load of flat-books in one arm, and a pair of poopy underpants in the other outstretched hand. She looks at me suspiciously—no fool.

"Frieda! Look who's here! Our new friend who lives across the street—she loves to read books. Would you like to sit on her lap? Show her your books. Frieda, show your new friend the book you want her to read to you."

Frieda, sensibly enough, it seems to me, is reluctant to park her wet little butt on some stranger's lap, sensing, as she must, the stranger's severely limited enthusiasm for such a project. Her parents are undaunted, however, and say, "Do you need to go potty? Do you want to show your new friend your potty? She wants to see it."

Her new friend once raised a family of her own. She does not remember that long-ago process as one which required an audience of attentive strangers, much less their participation in the celebration of a family member's digestive functions. Things must be different in Cambridge.

"Come on, then, we'll all go," they tell Frieda. And dutifully I rise from the table and follow my new neighbors into their crowded living room, where they keep a red-and-yellow plastic potty chair, next to a beat-up harpsichord and a large pile of dirty laundry. I scan the bookshelves when they are not looking, to see what I can learn. The shelves are full of the earnest reading which they began in college, thirty years before, and apparently continue: Robert Coles, Carl Jung, Rollo May, the Sufi masters, illustrated collections of folktales from Africa and Native America, yellowed paperback copies of Hermann Hesse and Beckett and the nineteenth-century Russians, plus the usual smattering of books on witchcraft, bicycle repair, and the lost drawings of Egon Schiele.

On a table at the end of a battered sofa is the library of child-rearing advice. And a little shoebox full of felt-tipped markers, for the exercise of nascent graphic skills upon the surfaces of newly whitewashed walls.

Frieda twirls around on the heels of her cowboy boots

like a tiny soiled dervish. "Oh maybe we need to get dressed first," says Mommy. Frieda grabs her father by the leg and voices her opposition to this plan. "Take her, will you Chaz, and get some clothes on her?

"Do you want to get dressed?" asks Daddy.

She would rather not.

"Let's go look for your mermaid shirt. Can you help me look for your mermaid shirt?"

Frieda and her father disappear into the dark recesses of their new house, and I ask how they are settling in. Apparently there is some hard adjustment required; they have left friends and colleagues and food co-ops behind. As a result they feel a bit adrift, not yet anchored firmly to the rocks of this strange place. And their fears are centered, as is natural, upon their tiny daughter who will bear the brunt of this exile.

"We're so glad you came over today," my new neighbor says. "Frieda was very excited when we told her she was going to have a new favorite aunt. And we're so pleased to have somebody we feel comfortable leaving her with." This all comes as news to me. I was under the impression that I was being asked over on a Sunday morning to drink coffee and answer simple questions about where to get a beach sticker and a dump permit. It did not occur to me that I had been selected—on what basis?—to become the generous, unencumbered older lady whose life henceforth would happily revolve around the developmental demands of the neighbor child.

"It's amazing the way she's just taken to you immediately. Frieda's usually very shy with strangers. But she likes you."

"She's a beautiful little girl."

"Isn't she! I thought that she should really be doing some baby modeling for commercials, but then we got involved with the move and all. Then her music teacher told us that she's making unusual progress on the recorder, which is fine for the fundamentals, but we need to switch her over to the oboe soon. And of course gymnastics. Look at that little body! With Chaz's schedule and mine, it will be so helpful to have you available to take her around."

I am beginning to dislike the innocent little darling almost as much as I believe I will forever dislike her parents. Who have not yet understood that here in town we raise our kids the best we can, and hope that their names don't turn up in the court news. We give them space and time to get into a little good clean trouble. We leave them alone. We feed them, we make sure their clothes are clean. And then we go off to our jobs at the Industrial Park or the hardware store, assuming that at some point our children will know enough to pick up some of the slack.

Our kids do not get most of the advantages which we would give them if we could.

But on the other hand, it does not occur to them that firewood stacks itself, or that supper buys itself with its own money, and lays itself down on clean plates when we are hungry.

The qualities which they will develop as a result of their raggedy childhoods will make them kind, plainspoken, hardworking adults.

Who will be either invisible or alien to little Frieda when she meets them again in the package store or the gas station on some brief visit back to town.

Block Dance

I HEAR MUSIC FROM up the street, filtered through full stands of wild grape and poison ivy and all the other drapery of deep summer. I am alone in the parlor. It is Saturday night. I am trying to sit still enough to avoid working up a sweat which would dampen the clean clothes I put on after supper.

The wet heavy air is not a good conductor of sound. Nevertheless I hear the block dance a half mile away. The windows are open, of course, but between me and the falling-down tennis courts of the Driftwood Beach Improvement Association there are houses and barking dogs and a stream of traffic headed up the Neck. It surprises me to hear everything so clearly, so close. And it surprises me that I had forgotten that the block dance was this weekend.

I should have been paying attention, but it slipped away from me. I think this is a good sign. It means I had forgotten to feel sorry for myself in advance. Forgotten to worry about whether I would moon around the periphery of the party, feeling like a shipwrecked creature too long at sea. Trying to remember how to fit in with those whose lives are still ashore, intact.

I know that everyone has a hard fist of sorrow which grabs them when they least expect it. This is what makes a party the fine, brave thing it is. We dance when there will be people missing. We celebrate with the others, who all have reasons of their own to stay home from the block dance and brood.

And we're just rehearsing, anyway.

Because they hold a block dance *every* Saturday night in heaven. No one stays home and watches sad TV. No one does laundry or tries to read a book.

They play old 45's. Everybody does the twist, the swim, the lindy hop. Angels hover around behind the picnic table where congo bars and Rice Krispies Treats are heaped up on paper plates. Angels are in charge of making sure the ice chests are always full of sodas.

Listen, beloved: you will be surprised some night to see me standing there in a pretty dress, underneath the colored lights. We'll slow dance to "Duke of Earl." We'll wrap our arms around each other on the short walk home, and in the morning stay in bed til noon.

Tall Ships

I WAS ALWAYS CARSICK, until I learned to drive—apparently it has to do with control. I still suffer from seasickness, but that is less of a problem, since my life no longer requires me to be on boats.

I particularly dislike sailboats, and have ever since that ill-considered first marriage into a yacht-clubby family had me spending most of the summers of my twenties somewhere off the Weepeckets, puking my lunch over the leeward rail.

Without this experience, of course, I wouldn't have a clue which rail was leeward, or why it mattered.

So the sight of tall ships in the bay does nothing for me. But every few years some organization with deep pockets and lots of international contacts rounds up the few surviving sail-powered military and commercial behemoths, and parades them up and down the coast from New York to New Hampshire and back.

And everyone around here goes into a tizzy. For a few days there are tall ships off the horizon, tall ships in the Canal, a tall ship from the former Soviet Union tied up at the Massachusetts Maritime Academy. Where all are free to go aboard and chat amiably in Russian with a crew of young men who apparently are immune to nausea, and who enjoy pretending that it is 1860 and that the czar's idea of full employment is conscription for life. Which may be a brief hitch anyway, since penicillin and anesthesia have not yet been invented. To say nothing of refrigeration, decent seagoing sanitation, or the Emergency Medical Airlift.

I am told that the sight of tall ships brings a shiver to the flesh, that it is glorious and proud and haunting to see so much canvas flying over a huge wooden hull. I am certain that you would tell me I have ice water in my veins, where you have salt. You understand what I do not—something about the ghosts of a time long gone, when men were men and the sea was their inheritance.

"Exactly!" I would answer back, remembering all the peanut butter and jelly sandwiches I threw up in a former life. Which then floated past me on their way to Georges Bank.

Auntie

I̲t's impossible to know, of course, whose death will leave the biggest hole, the deepest silence in the world. But I have lived here long enough to have figured out that the smart money doesn't bet on the sleekest horses. Because here in Weweantic, at least, the race is seldom to the swift.

One day I was standing in a long line at Wal-Mart, waiting to check out. The joint was full of tourists who had forgotten to bring their nice manners with them from home. Most of them were clearly annoyed to be in the middle of so much compressed humanity; it hadn't occurred to them that the scarcity of parking spaces near the store, and the shortage of clerks to show them where to find the ant buttons, are seasonal phenomena. Of which they compose the largest part.

That all this isn't *our* fault.

In any event, I heard a man behind me say, "Look at that woman—she's just plain pathetic." I was pretty sure he wasn't referring to me, although I'm as likely a candidate as anyone else. I turned around to sneak a look at him and his equally impatient wife. And then I scanned the crowd for an example of pathos beyond the standards which I myself am able to set. I didn't see anything out of the ordinary. A bunch of locals. Familiar faces. Nobody bobbing about sorrowfully in the churning sea of out-of-towners.

"Look at her. Why doesn't she *do* something to herself."

And I followed his eyes to the lady ahead of me, whose name I don't know, but whose face I do. A woman in a house-dress. Who wears white tube socks and men's shoes on her swollen legs and feet. Who walks with great difficulty on painful hip joints which in a perfect world would have already been surgically replaced. Who does not smell as fresh as I would wish, whose short hair sticks up in greasy spikes. And who I often see at the grocery store, engaged in acts of petty larceny.

We meet frequently at the stale rack. Where we discuss the relative merits of the dried-out baked goods; where I ignore her tendency to open up the bags and poke at all the dough-nuts. She doesn't seem the slightest bit unusual, or at least she is not beyond the range of normal here. There are lots of us who might stick out like sore swollen diabetic thumbs in some other town. Lucky for us that we live here.

So while I stood in line I devoted a little time to thinking hateful thoughts about the man behind me.

Which made me feel guilty, right away. And so, instead, I thought about Auntie, who's been gone for almost twenty years, and how useful she would be in this situation.

I've been told that Auntie, when young, was a woman of staggering beauty. That she had worked for years as a stripper in one of the less savory beachfront bars. Where she'd made a lot of money. She invested some of it in real estate—a couple of little cottages in the seediest part of town—and kept the rest in cash under her bed. By the time I knew her she was an imposing old woman of regal bearing and proportion, with the disposition of a snapping turtle.

A stroke had stilled one half of her huge body. Parkinson's disease had grabbed hold of the other side, dancing it around. She could no longer drive, but she could hitchhike, sticking out a wildly palsied hand to beg for rides.

At least it seemed like begging to the new people in town. They saw a fierce-eyed old lady who looked exactly like Queen Liliuokalani, standing on the side of the road in polyester shorts and flip-flops. An old lady who would stick her head in the open window of their cars, and demand to be taken to Fall River.

It frightened them, of course. With good reason. Auntie would get in the car and then she would not get out. Any stranger generous or foolhardy enough to acquiesce to her demands would find that they were in for the duration.

But the new people, once they were past their initial fear of the rest of us, wanted very much to show that they could fit right in. So one day, while stopped at a red light in front of the railroad tracks downtown, they would be accosted by an old lady who said she needed a ride to the doctor's. They would accept the job with an oily sense of mission. And the squeamishness of a fraternity pledge about to eat a bug. They would lean over to open the passenger side door, before noticing that Auntie had already begun to settle herself into the broad expanse of the backseat.

Hours and hours later—sometimes in the evening of a long hard day—they would knock on our back door and want to tell us about the lunatic old lady hitchhiker who had refused to get out of their car. Who did not want to get to a doctor's appointment at all, and had commandeered the vehicle, and forced them to drive and drive and drive. "Oh," we'd tell them, "that was Auntie. If it bothers you, just ignore her next time. Let someone else pick her up."

The new people would laugh nervously, palpably relieved.

Because not only had they survived the experience, and felt themselves now part of local life, but they mistakenly believed that they had also been given permission to think of Auntie as a cartoon character, one more small-town eccentric, someone to talk about when asked by friends back home about how they were adjusting to the move away from Beacon Hill.

This uncooperative old lady had a given name, of course, like anyone else; Auntie was an honorific. One which she had earned the hard way, over time. The new people must have supposed that it was a nickname, a mild antique racial slur. Nothing could have been further from the truth. Auntie had never married. She had used the money she earned at night, peeling off her clothes, to raise up dozens and dozens of children no one else could take. Generations of Weweantic policemen and teachers and fishermen and laborers and mail carriers had grown up in Auntie's spotless home. She'd sent more than a few away to college, on the money tucked underneath the mattress. When she died there was still money left which went to pay tuition for a couple of dozen more.

Lots of people miss her terribly.

So when the creep behind me in line at Wal-Mart begins to entertain himself with a clever game of Spot The Freaks, I wish that Auntie could be here. We need her to stand outside in the parking lot and wait for him. We need her to listen for the sound of the remote control which unlocks the doors of his SUV. And in that slow moment before he knows what's happening, we need her to crawl into the cool backseat, and spread herself out comfortably. And demand that he drive her up and down Route 495, all day and deep into the starry darkness of the summer night. From Weweantic to the Rhode Island border and back. Over and over and over. Until he and his wife are exhausted and there is silence everywhere, except for the rustle of Auntie's palsied hand, and—from the front seat—the sound of desperate, muffled sobbing.

The ATM

I BELIEVE I HAVE been touched by an angel. It has not been my first experience with unexplainable kindness in an otherwise random universe. But it was my first confrontation with unseen forces whose day jobs are even more tedious than my own.

An ATM card came in the mail a few months ago. I've never had an ATM card before, but our little local bank was bought out by a big bank, which came in and made some changes. First they put up migrainously floral new wallpaper, and then they brought an ATM machine to town. They sent me a plastic card, and suggested in the strongest possible terms that I learn to use it.

It has been unsettling. The old regime knew me well enough to understand the limited usefulness of a debit card to

someone whose bank balance is frequently in the single dig-
its. There are plenty of us here in the same leaky boat, who
don't need a way to withdraw a minimum of ten whole dollars.
We have the grocery store to write checks that we know we
can't cover for forty-eight hours. We think of the IGA as a financial institution which also sells milk. The old bank never made
a fuss about any of this. But the new bank would like us to do
better. According to the frequent promotional mailings I get
from them, they care very deeply about our well-being, and our
ability to keep up with things.

So I went down to the bank to activate my card, and dis-
covered that the ATM isn't anywhere near the bank itself. You
probably know already all about these things, but it came as
news to me that the bright blue box at the weedy edge of the
hardware store parking lot is where we are supposed to go now
to deal with hard financial reality.

I went and stood in front of the thing, surrounded by a
tangle of goldenrod and wild purple asters. A silent movie was
running on a tiny screen, which I watched until I understood
what was expected of me.

Then the machine began to speak. "Look carefully at your
available options," it said, in the unmistakable voice of someone born and raised in Belfast. "Then make a choice."

I was dumbfounded. And made the thing repeat itself,
over and over, until I understood what it was telling me: *Think,
plan, then do the best you can.*

What I do not understand is why some poor winged creature has to spend her days inside the confines of something the
size of a portable toilet, or why no one else in town has noticed
that our ATM dispenses profoundly rational and useful and
comforting life advice in the sweet voice of someone from the
North of Ireland.

I can only assume that I am not the only one who lives
such a cheerfully spirit-ridden life, and that the angel in the
box sounds like Cape Verde or Poland or Barbados or even
Weweantic, Massachusetts, depending on the customer.

White Peaches

I DROVE OUT TO Acushnet this week with a friend to buy white peaches. She's a townie and knows where all the skeletons are buried and when the peaches will be ripe.

Acushnet is where heaven buys its sweetcorn and cut flowers. It is where the green beans come from that the saints eat for lunch, alongside fresh broiled scup caught off the beaches one town over.

There is no ocean in Acushnet. You can feel the presence of the sea, but you are beyond the summer cottages and taffy stands. The place is mostly cows and cranberry bogs beside long empty stretches of country road.

It is late for white peaches. White peaches are a fragile local delicacy which smell faintly of raspberries. They bruise

easily. They are fussy and undependable and unspeakably deli-
cious. They ripen first, before the hardier yellows. They are not
for sale in grocery stores, of course. One must drive out to
Achusnet for expensive white peaches. And one must depend
on word of mouth to know when they are ready.

On this particular day my friend and I drove past one
immaculately maintained orchard after another. On an isolated
rise sits a tiny Quaker meetinghouse surrounded by the trees
which belong to *my* favorite orchard. She told me to keep
going.

We finally pulled into the driveway of a dilapidated farm-
house. The shutters were down on the produce stand out front.
It was too early in the day for them to have sold out, so I assumed that whoever worked this land must be in the fields
picking, or doing some other hot thankless job on a muggy day
at the end of summer.

"There he is!" my friend said. "He sold me the last of his
white peaches yesterday." I was confused. Why were we here, if
all the peaches were gone?

She ran over to a rusted pickup truck parked in the shade.
A scruffy guy with a day's growth of beard was slumped in the
front seat. He looked about my age. I jumped out to hear what
was being said.

"No peaches today. I'm too hung over to pick, " he told
us. "God. I feel awful."

"You told me there'd be drops," my friend reminded him. He looked at her like she was about to administer some kind of primitive electroshock therapy.

He got slowly and painfully out of his truck. "I'm too hung over to work," he said to me. "I was out all night drinking and I'm sick as a dog."

"Down at the Bar-Bee-Q Ranch?" I asked. The Bar-Bee-Q Ranch is a good place to get drunk for not much money. It's up the street, between a field of cow corn and a stand of apple trees.

"God no. I go drink where no one knows me."

"How far do you have to go to accomplish that?" I asked, thinking that he seemed like a decent enough guy. "Vermont?"

He laughed, and stood looking at us for a minute. He lit a cigarette with shaking hands, and disappeared back into the darkness of the shuttered farm stand. He came out with two boxes of white peaches he'd hidden underneath a couple of sawhorses in a back corner.

"You ladies want these peaches?"

Yes indeed. We did. The last two boxes of white peaches. He took our money and crawled back into his truck, ashen faced, and tried to wave goodbye with unsteady hands in the unforgiving heat.

We were almost over the town line before she said, "He liked you, you know. Frank's been wicked sick and shaky for the last few years, but if you'd made his mistakes you'd be shaky too."

"Good Lord, what did he do?"

She laughed. "A few years back when cranberries were up around eighty-three dollars a barrel, he cut down four acres of white peaches and turned them into bogs. And now cranberries are down to about eighty-three *cents* for crying out loud. No wonder he goes where nobody knows him to drink himself sick."

"But he liked you," she said, smiling her calculating old smile. "I could tell."

Therapists in August

W E'RE ALL DEPRESSED. IN spite of pro-
paganda put out by the Commonwealth's Department of Tourism, the seashore in August is a damp, ruinously fog-swamped
place where the only comfort is at the Mall. The sun which
cheered and calmed us in June and glorious July will not be
visible all month. And to make matters worse, our mail is full
of flyers from Target and the Payless shoe store, reminding us
that it won't be long before school starts up again.

But, as everyone knows, you can't have an existential
crisis in the month of August because all the therapists are
on vacation. These strange but indispensable people might
choose any time of year to sit alone beside the ocean. Yet they
go off and leave us for the moldy confines of Martha's Vineyard

when it is certain there will be unremitting spells of overcast and furious rain.

Just when we are filled with dread.

Although it has been decades since we ourselves were the ones in need of new gym sneakers, we are nevertheless riven with anxiety. We walk the freshly stocked aisles of notebook paper, backpacks, and three-ring binders, pretending to have come in for a fresh supply of felt-tip pens. We test ourselves against the pegboard walls of plastic rulers, pencil cases, and erasers in the shape of Japanese anime characters. We look at all the packages of stickers, trying to decide which would be the best to trade with during recess; which would give us enough advantage in the political turmoil of third grade to guarantee that we would not end up eating lunch alone.

Meanwhile, on the porches of their rented summer houses, the psychiatrists sit with all the books they meant to read last winter. The greens are too wet for golf. It's too choppy on the bay to sail. Or it's becalmed. Either way, there they are, for the whole month of August. And there's no one left for us to talk to.

About the difficulty we have finishing our homework. About our fear of getting on the bus. What if the teacher doesn't like us?

What if we don't get another chance?

All the therapists are drinking vodka gimlets in late afternoon. From what I know of summer houses in the nasty heat and drizzle of the closing weeks of August, they can't be having what I would recognize as fun. We find it hard to understand why they wouldn't rather be back at the office, returning our calls.

Meanwhile we are stranded at home with our shorts in a twist, worrying that in September we might find ourselves back in cheesy knock-offs, carrying a cafeteria tray. And at the same time we are inexplicably sad to know that we will not.

The psychiatrists are happy just to be away from us. It will be a month before they come back and explain to us why we do not feel relieved when we remember that all our book reports are finished. That all our homework has been handed in.

It will be a month before they come back and explain to us why this news should cause such perverse sorrow.

The Queen Mum's Cake

I SPEND THE MORNING baking a cake for the Queen Mum's birthday. I am a few weeks late for the celebration of the actual date of this venerable woman's birth, but every year I have to wait for a day when it's cool enough to turn on the oven.

Air-conditioning is not an option in this house. The long-ago Colonials who built the place cut more than a few corners. The support beams, which hold everything up, are merely felled trees with the bark left on. After centuries of insect predation the floors are wide pine board trampolines, which frighten people who don't know how to walk around the spongy places where there isn't any furniture. Other things have fallen into disrepair out of plain neglect, for which I can't blame the Colonists. The wiring is one of those problematic areas which is my fault, not theirs. Either way, though, it means I have to be careful.

So I wait until I wake to an unexpectedly fine morning in late summer to bake the Queen Mum's birthday cake. Some fine bright day with a lovely breeze. A day when the kitchen will fill with the smell of saltwater and someone else's freshly cut grass. I get out the cake recipe which my mother gave me, after she found it misfiled under "Piccalillis." It's typed out on cheap manila paper which long ago turned the color of good caramel. And is folded into quadrants held together with caramel-colored Scotch tape.

"Queen Elizabeth's Cake," the recipe says. "This is the only cake that the Queen makes herself. She goes into her own kitchen to stir this up." The Queen Mum Elizabeth. This is a relic of the War Effort.

It is a plain, abstemious little cake. It requires me to soak one cup of chopped dates in boiling water. I do not particularly like chopped dates. But I *am* fond of the Queen Mum.

This is a faintly heretical opinion to hold, almost anywhere in New England. We have not forgotten who whipped those Red Coat butts from here to Liverpool, only twelve or thirteen generations ago. An unspoken resignation and disappointment lingers in the air here when certain old Yankees think of Canada. As if we had lacked the political will to finish what we started.

But mention Dunkirk, and even the least forgiving old salt

gets misty-eyed. And good reason for it, too. We would all like to think that we would also have the courage to set off together in battered lobster boats and beautifully maintained wooden gaff-rigged day sailers and the odd party boat to rescue our loved ones hopelessly trapped on an enemy beach. Rich and poor together. We would like to think that inherited privilege makes no difference when there is work to do.

So I bake the cake, which is not particularly remarkable as cakes go, but does come with a royal command: "This recipe is not to be passed on but must be sold for charitable purposes for fifteen cents." I calculate that after sixty years of inflation this comes to a dollar eighty-four. I fill an envelope with pennies, and drop my one hundred and eighty-four mites into the kettle at the Salvation Army.

Every year, though, while the cake is cooling on the counter, I am reminded why we have not entirely forgiven the old European monarchists. I am forced to hustle around in the heat, swabbing up the gummy mess I've made with flour and real butter and one beaten egg.

This is a chore from which I assume even in wartime the Queen Mum was excused.

Some Random Thoughts
on the Subject of Love:
I Corinthians 13

I T WOULDN'T MATTER IF I could speak all the languages of men and angels—if I didn't love other people I'd just sound like the background music on the old Gong Show.

Or I could have enough presence to convince a public radio audience of the need for universal health care and a serious ratcheting-up of the currently deplorable level of the minimum wage, to the point of thinking I could single-handedly change domestic policy—but if I didn't love other people then I'd just be some self-righteous old broad with access to the big microphone.

Or I could sell everything I own and give the money to a homeless shelter, and then fast for social justice on the Capitol steps until I finally died of exposure—but if I didn't love other people I wouldn't get points for any of it.

Love is patient. Kind. It doesn't make Top Ten lists. Doesn't watch itself admiringly from across the street.

Love has learned when to keep its damned mouth shut. It tries to remember to cut the poor benighted suckers on the other side some slack.

Love doesn't dish the dirt, even the really good stuff involving sex, stupidity, and hard evidence. It prefers the kind of stories where some plucky soul overcomes terrible obstacles and Triumphs Nicely Over Adversity.

Love doesn't break. It keeps on believing, keeps on hoping, and keeps on keepin' on.

Love has some kind of physics-defying permanence. Celebrity, on the other hand, will implode; poetry and art will fall under the weight of Post-Modernism; knowledge will evolve from overload into impenetrability.

We are, all of us, in the habit of formulating breathtaking hypotheses from hilariously insufficient data.

Someday we'll figure it all out. We'll have a Unified Field Theory of Everything. Except that none of it will be theoretical.

When I was a kid my tastes and opinions were just the teeniest bit jejune. Eventually I grew up and got over myself.

Right now we try to see the face of The Imaginer, and all we have are mirrors. Someday there will be a window.

In the meantime, what makes it possible for us to get up in the morning is an uninterrupted supply of decency, courage, and love. And it's love, of course, which gets us through the day.

Putting Something By

I N SUMMER, OLD GUYS set up card tables in the shade beside the road and spend the day sitting next to a display of whatever is ripe. They drive out to where we are likely to pass by on our way home from work. They bring a folding chair, a thermos of coffee, and every now and then a swollen, battered paperback to pass the time—although they prefer conversation to the printed word.

Early in the season there are strawberries, of course. Somebody else did the picking—strawberries require kneeling painfully across the rows; it's a job for little kids. Assuming they can be convinced to avoid kneeling on the fruit itself.

Then there is a slow month before the garden crops come in. The old guys pile their tables with sweetcorn which only the

summer people stop to buy. We know it isn't local corn—
it can't be. The rule for a successful stand of corn in New
England has, for centuries, been *"knee high by the Fourth of
July."* Anything you get your hands on from June to late August
has been trucked up from Florida. And passed off to city people as brand-new sweetcorn only hours from the stalk.

Eventually the tables fill with honest tomatoes and nice
slender pea pods and bait buckets full of gladiolas. This is
when I begin to get interested, and will pull over to look at the
pickling cukes.

Then, when it is too hot to care about anything after work
except a swim and a change of clothes, the fruit ripens. All
at once. The old guys set out pints of blueberries and grapes
and apricots and nectarines. Raspberries. Blackberries. Crab
apples, cherries, plums. All of it seductive and insistent. All of
it fragile and soon gone.

Of course you know that this cannot be absolutely true:
everything cannot ripen at the same time. It couldn't work that
way; even the greedy birds and rapacious hordes of backyard
deer could not eat their way through that much fruit. The fruit
long ago learned to space itself out a bit, in order to have a
decent chance of riding through some animal's intestine. But
when I come across the folding tables set out with pint boxes
of seed wrapped in delight, at the end of a hot tired day, deep
in the muggy part of summer, it's overwhelming. I feel the pres-

sure of abundance. The weight of knowing how brief the season is for certain pleasures. The necessity of putting something by for winter.

It becomes almost too much to ask of me.

But I drag home whole flats of fruit anyway, because of the importance of making jelly. When Aubrey was alive I did this as a form of performance art. He loved the idea of it, as if cooking up jelly was an arcane skill, some kind of backroads wizardry. Didn't they have blueberries in Brooklyn? Apparently not. He would come home all excited with the backseat full of something sweet and ripe—on the most miserably hot days in summer—so that we could cook up a batch of jam. His job was to sit and drink tea and smile at me fondly while I stained the front of my shirt. My job was to put on a good show.

The memory of those hot afternoons stabs at me now, wishing hard, as I pick the stems off a zillion grapes, that I had my old audience with me now.

The process is uncomplicated but time-consuming. You wash the fruit. You dump it in your biggest pot—the one you also use to tie-dye shirts. You set this on the stove, and turn up the heat. It will be suffocating in the kitchen, even though early in the day you thought to pull the shades against the worst of the murky green sun. You wait for the berries to move and squeak. You pay close attention to the steam that rises from the bursting skins. Eventually the fruit gives up and turns to mush.

You pour the slurry through a sieve. What comes out gets strained again, dripping undisturbed through a couple of folds of cheesecloth. Meanwhile you boil the jars and lids. This makes them safe and sterile, after a year spent sitting empty in a dusty box. At this point you are dripping wet. You wipe your face on a damp apron, and take a deep breath.

Then you measure out the rest of the ingredients. You stop to get the recipe straight in your head. Because from here it happens fast.

You bring everything to a rolling boil. At which point the sugar, acid, and pectin fuse. Stirring hard, you count out sixty Mississippis. Then take it off the heat.

You fish the jars out of the boiling water. You drain them for a second, upside down on a clean dishtowel. Then you fill them—quickly! And cap them and screw the band on gently, not too tight. You wipe them dry. Then line them up on all the windowsills to cool. Where the light shines through them, too pretty to be real.

One by one the lids begin to snap down tight. You hear them chirp like crickets in the dark.

It was our fondest wish that we might be old together. If Aubrey had lived, he certainly would have become, by now, one of the geezers with folding tables full of fruit. I always check when I go by a station wagon parked in the shade. Just in case.

There is no longer any reason, practical or theatrical, for making jelly in the deep-canyon afternoons of summer. The stuff from stores is cheap and good. But certain hungers do not fade with age. There are cravings which are not diminished over time.

So I continue to put something by. In order to guarantee— now as then—that some cold morning in the otherwise un-knowable future I'll be reminded of the heat.

The sweetness will remind me.

The Ladies Who
Swim at Suppertime

I'VE BECOME ONE OF the ladies who swim at suppertime. Who go down to the public beach when the sun is low against the horizon and the parking lot is empty. Who leave our purses on the front seat of the car, and drop a faded bath towel near the water's edge. Then walk our puffy old bodies into the buoyant saltwater, where we paddle around until we feel the stiffness leave the sore places in our joints and muscles. Until the vague anxiety of late afternoon is washed off of our loosening flesh, and out into the bay.

None of us believes wholeheartedly that we are not the slender girls who once laughed and swam in little two-piece cotton bathing suits in the full warm light of midday. Or one of the young mothers chasing babies on the beach.

I suppose that none of us expected to live long enough

to be one of the thick-waisted women with knobby feet, whose bathing costumes cover as much of us as possible. We would wear full-length trench coats if we could get away with it, and some of us fantasize about the theoretical possibilities of a Cone of Invisibility. Until some saintly physicist figures out how to build an affordable waterproof prototype, we are stuck with our ridiculous old-lady bathing suits with navy blue skirts. Attached to polyester tops with completely inadequate internal bracing. Sometimes we add useless rubber bathing caps, the kind that strap under our accumulating chins.

No matter. The place is deserted, except for us. The lifeguards have gone home. The sand is full of tiny footprints and dissolving sand castles, but the minivans have loaded up and headed back. Their occupants are busy getting food on the table. Changing diapers, throwing loads of wet towels and bathing suits into the washing machine, marshaling the troops.

Which is when we take their places on the public beach at sunset. The wind drops. We walk quickly into the surf, knowing that at this time of year the ocean will be as warm as the primordial soup.

We churn the water with our stout legs, and wonder: if we are no longer useful, and no longer decorative, what are we?

We bob around in the fading light until we begin to prune up. By that time we are limp and loose. We are prehistoric jellyfish. We are floating beds of kelp.

Then, when we have regained some sense of geologic time, the kind required to pound the edges of a continent into fine white sand, we stand up. We take one last look at the horizon and the distant, unseen shore. We climb heavily and slowly out of the water, surprised by the pull of gravity.

Back to our cars, where we put our damp towel down on the upholstery, as if that would do any good. We have to drive home past all the houses full of dinner and life and noise. But it doesn't matter. Our swim has left us as placid and untroubled as an ice cube, melting quietly on the floor of the back porch.

Acknowledgments

I WISH TO ACKNOWLEDGE my deep love and gratitude to Jay Allison and Victoria Merrick, who pulled me from deep water and into the boat. This little book exists because of them, and is in great measure a product of their intellects and hearts. The weak spots are my own; the elevated portions of this work belong to them.

And also to my editor, Emily Loose. Who was willing to show me where I had fallen short of my intention, and who was always careful to point me home.

I am grateful beyond words to my agent Jonathon Lazear.

To Noah Adams and Neenah Ellis.

To Ellen Weiss.

To Art Silverman.

To the staff of public radio stations WCAI/WNAN in Woods Hole, Massachusetts, and WGBH in Boston.

To everyone at National Public Radio. Upon which so much depends.

Finally, I wish to thank Elaine Mello, who, before any of this happened, made it possible for me and so many others to stay afloat until help arrived.

About the Author

Carol Wasserman is a regular commentator on National Public Radio's "All Things Considered". In 1998, she was named a Poetry Fellow by the Massachusetts Cultural Council.